WHAT OTHERS ARE SAYING
ABOUT *AUTHENTIC*

A whole generation of Christians need to read this book. Rob Reimer comforts and confronts those who are looking for honesty and authenticity in their Christian life. Many living in passive compliance to external traditions, rules, and cultures in their walk with God, yet having a deep desire for more, will find here biblical patterns and principles to freedom and growth in Christ. This work challenges and encourages us to a deeper authentic journey—for the partisan, pupil, preacher, or proclaimer of faith in Christ.

    —**REV. KEN GRAHAM,** *President, Christian and Missionary Alliance of Australia*
    Regional Coordinator, Asia Pacific Alliance Churches AWF

Will the Master sign a work that is not His?

Would a canvas bear the autograph of one who is not behind its design? Would an artist sign a poster copy of his masterwork? Will a master be told what his masterpiece should display?

No. These works are not authentic.

It is this examination of authenticity that Dr. Rob Reimer challenges you to undertake in *Authentic*, a litmus test for the soul. In it, his curated questions cut through artifice to reveal the motives and posture of the heart.

Paradoxically calloused by a culture of grace defined by unmerited favor, we have forgotten the truth that grace is divine influence on our heart and its reflection in our life. The application of Dr. Reimer's *Authentic* reveals that, for so many of us, the hallmarks and structure of a great work may be on display, but the canvas lacks the Master's brushstrokes.

With his trademark transparency, in *Authentic* Dr. Reimer joins you on a journey, beckoning you from life in the outer court, to deep inside the temple, to discover that the veil was rent for a reason. It is his heart that you encounter this reason for yourself, doing so in the presence and intimacy of an abiding relationship with a loving Father, without impediment.

For the reader, it is crucial to remain in sync with the author, walking slowly. Quick checkmarks for yourself, or thinking the questions apply to others, mean you have wandered off the path.

It's only through this internal journey that we move beyond a life bearing the Christian signature to becoming an authentic, unique, and purposefully designed masterpiece that brings glory to the Artist.

—**ELIZABETH HOPKINS**, *journalist*

As a recovering elder brother, this book caused me to pause several times as it frankly addressed my behavioral religious defaults. Ouch. In his straightforward way, Rob lays out, in *Authentic*, how to freely and humbly live in intimacy with Jesus. It is a beautiful reminder that God's grace is available to all who receive it by faith.

—**WANDA WALBORN**, *author of* Spiritual Journey: Can I Really Get Close to God?
Director of Empower, a developmental program for women

In *Authentic*, Rob has highlighted and unpacked something that has hampered many churches for many seasons.

Using probing and disarming questions, Rob opens a conversation and challenges the mindset that is quenching so many churches: the rituals of religion.

Rob believes and calls us all to believe what Jesus said: "When you receive the Holy Spirit, you will receive power and love." *Authentic* challenges and encourages us to believe, trust, and act differently, through having an authentic relationship with the Father, Son, and Holy Spirit and authentically loving people.

Along with challenging our thinking and actions, Rob also gives practical ways to pursue God and have an authentic relationship with Him.

If you are looking to know your heavenly Father more deeply and experience a truly authentic relationship with Him, let this book take you on a journey of discovery of renewed love and faith that will change how you live and do church.

—**JOHN HUTCHINSON**, *Executive Minister*
Churches of Christ in Western Australia

My friend Dr. Rob Reimer has done it again: he has written a book that will impact you to the core and transform your walk with God! *Authentic* is a transformative masterpiece that intricately weaves together profound spiritual truths and practical insights to guide readers on a journey toward a deeper, more authentic relationship with God. Through compelling narratives, Dr. Reimer skillfully navigates the complexities of faith, urging us to move beyond mere religious routines to embrace a life supernaturally empowered by the Holy Spirit. I found myself challenged throughout to go deeper into an "authentic" relationship and not to be content with my routines that may no longer be working. This book is a light in a world yearning for genuine encounters with the living God. I wholeheartedly endorse *Authentic* as a must read for anyone seeking to cultivate a vibrant, transformative, and deeply intimate connection with God.

—**RON EIVAZ,** *Senior Pastor, Harvest Church*
(harvestonline.church)
Founder and Apostolic Overseer, Harvest Ministry Network
(hmnetwork.org)

The church in America is plagued by many challenges in this cultural moment. Chief among them is that many have exchanged actual encounter with God for religious activity, human systems, or self-delusion, all of which leaves them empty and alone. I'm so grateful for Rob's work in *Authentic* which calls out so much of the "fake" religion in our churches and lives that leads to bondage and disconnect from God. But then, Rob doesn't just leave us depressed; he offers hope and a pathway forward to a genuine, deep, and power-filled life with Jesus that would spur the church to revival and renewal. I hope many people read this book and feel liberated from control, fear, and performance and are drawn to authentic life in Christ.

—**TIM MEIER,** *Vice President for Development, Christian and Missionary Alliance*

I have just finished reading my friend Rob Reimer's new book, *Authentic*, for the second time. Rob hungers for genuine encounters with the manifest presence of God, and this book charts the path to those moments. The book rings true because Rob is authentic. I probably know him better than any of you reading this (except Jen), and I can say that what you see and read is real and true. Rob is an authentic man of integrity. May this book birth a generation of authentic followers of Jesus!

—**RON WALBORN**, *D. Min., Executive Director of Urban Initiatives, Asbury Seminary (NY)*
Asbury Theological Seminary

I've noticed that whenever I ask for more of God, He asks more from me. God wants us to enjoy thriving and intimate fellowship with Him. Rob Reimer often says, "You can have as much of God as you want, but not more than you're willing to pay the price for." In his new book, Dr. Reimer invites us to experience God in a more profound way than we ever have before. In the process, he lovingly confronts our tendency to phone it in, disengage, and go through the motions. He also challenges our instinct to pretend, and the pride that resists a fresh work of the Spirit. God wants more from us. God has more for us. Take your time reading this book. Ponder, pray, and reflect on what God wants to say to you in this season of your life. May you sense God's very personal invitation to you. May you cultivate a lifestyle of listening for His voice. Lean in as you read this book. The pages are flourishing with wisdom. If you long for a personal revival, this message is for you.

—**SUSIE LARSON**, *Talk radio host, national speaker*
Bestselling author
Host, Susie Larson Live
Faith Radio, myfaithradio.com

Authentic not only gives us clarity on what we truly desire but introduces us to capital "A" Authentic, Jesus. This message is so essential, and quite compelling, to the emerging generations who are sick of the fake, flimsy, and flashy and just want real and authentic. Rob has prophetically poked at the church and its disciples again—and I am grateful.

—**ZACH MEERKREEBS**, *Pastor-in-Residence, Asbury University*

AUTHENTIC

Cultivating Authentic
Relationship with God

Dr. Rob Reimer

Carpenter's Son Publishing

Published by Carpenter's Son Publishing, Franklin, Tennessee
ClovercroftPublishingGroup.com

Cover Design by Darcy Reimer

Edited by Robert Irvin

Interior Design by Suzanne Lawing

Printed in the United States of America

ISBN: 978-1-956370-50-8 (print)

CONTENTS

Introduction

FROM LEARNED BEHAVIORS TO AUTHENTIC EXPERIENCE

Think about the season of your life when you connected with God most deeply. When was it you felt His love the strongest, heard His voice the clearest, experienced His presence the deepest? I remember the first time I experienced Jesus in a significant way. It was after a breakup with a girlfriend in college, and I had a life-altering encounter with the risen Christ. I felt His overwhelming love. Then, years later, I remember experiencing Jesus deeply in the midst of a crisis in the early years of my marriage with Jen. I experienced God's voice, His sustaining presence, His daily strength, His tender compassion, and His transformational work. I remember the time I began to hunger and thirst for God's presence, when I longed for more.

I sought God with all my heart in seasons of prayer, fasting, retreating, and prayer watching through the night. And God met me in amazing ways. I was living in the floodgate of God's presence. I could write about many deep seasons I have had with God. Thinking back on these times makes my heart long for more of God. I don't want to lose the passionate edge, the palpable presence, of God in my life. I don't want to settle for the mundane, the routine, or the ruts of religion. I want the authentic. I don't just want to know about God; I want to know Him deeply and personally. I want to experience more of His love, presence, and power. I want to hear Him more clearly, follow Him more closely, and honor Him more completely. I want to draw near to God in real and authentic intimacy.

One of the problems with being a Christ-follower is we can substitute religious expressions for authentic experiences and not even know we are doing it. We can start with significant, transformational, authentic encounters with God and end up with dusty old religion. We can lose contact with these real connections with God and look back on them with distant memory, wondering how we lost our way and how we get back to where we were. Or we can chalk them off as anomalies.

After that first encounter I had with God, I remember asking people about their spiritual journeys, if they had similar encounters. I asked them about experiences where they were filled with the Spirit. Many people told me about some encounter they had many years ago, but it was now a distant, twenty-year-old memory. When I asked about their current experiences with God, they were often left with a loss for words. They weren't living in the current fullness of the Spirit. They had a previous encounter they recalled with fondness, but they were now living in a bit of a spiritual desert. And sadly, they often talked with me as if that were the norm.

I think there are a multitude of reasons why we trade authentic encounters for religious activities. As Christians, sometimes we can end up doing all the right things for all the wrong reasons. We spend regular time alone with God, pray, and read our Bible every day, because that is what good

> We don't even notice the subtle slide. We keep doing the right thing, but we no longer draw near like we once did.

Christians are supposed to do. Over time our motivation for our spiritual practices morphs from moved by love to motivated by duty, and we don't even notice the subtle slide. We keep doing the right thing, but we no longer draw near like we once did. We keep on with the old activities, but we no longer have that fire burning in our hearts. When we continue to practice these disciplines devoid of the authentic encounters with Jesus that lead to deep, life-changing intimacy, our spiritual life often becomes dry and shallow. At other times we shift toward religion because our rhythm becomes tired. It was once fresh and powerful, but now it is stale and routine. We are still doing the same spiritual activities, but we're no longer seeing the results we once saw.

Still other times we move away from the authentic because we are carrying unprocessed pain. We are hurt and disappointed. We become a little distant from God because our trust has been undermined by life's pain. We still do what we once did because it has become our routine, but we no longer carry the trust, enthusiasm, and passion that used to characterize us. Sometimes we drift into the ruts of religion because we are busy doing so many things—good things, things with family, things at church, things for God—but we lose our first love for Jesus in the process of life's wearisome busyness.

Too often the problem is we are still doing the same things we were doing. So much is the same that it makes us feel like we are on the right track, but in reality we have lost our way.

We aren't doing bad things, but our hearts are drifting from Jesus. We are no longer passionate for Jesus like we were, and we are no longer encountering Him like we once did. We look back on those earlier days with gratitude and nostalgia, but they are fading into a distant memory. So many other people have the same story to tell, so we normalize it and, all the while, live beneath our potential.

We can be on this road toward religion and spiritual dryness . . . and not even know it, because we are doing the right spiritual things. We miss the subtle shift that has taken place in our hearts because there hasn't been a significant shift in our behaviors. Remember: the Pharisees read their Bible vigilantly, yet they killed Jesus. Their reading was full of knowledge but devoid of revelation. They learned all the right religious behaviors, engaged in all of the right spiritual disciplines—like fasting, praying, tithing, and Bible study—but they missed out on authentic, life-giving encounters with God. Somehow all their religious activity didn't lead them to the right outcome. Engaging in the right spiritual activities doesn't guarantee the right results. It could just make us religious and actually lead us far from God. It could leave us hard-hearted, judgmental, angry, and not like Jesus at all. How do we avoid simply being religious, and live a vibrant Christian life? How do we avoid substituting learned behaviors for authentic encounters?

One of the keys is to live an examined life. If we keep doing our regular routines without reflecting and inviting the Spirit to examine the condition of our heart, we will inevitably end up in the spiritual desert. Jesus said, "For out of the overflow of the heart the mouth speaks" (Matthew 12:34). The Proverb writer said, "Above all else, guard your heart, for everything you do flows from it" (Proverbs 4:23). An unguarded heart will never drift in a spiritually flourishing direction. A field left alone does not naturally move toward abundance; the law of entropy says the field will tend toward chaos. So it is with our souls. We need to take time before the Lord, and others, to live an examined life; we need to be sure we are doing the right things for the right reasons. This book will help you reflect on your life and help you root out any weedy entropy robbing you of spiritual fullness.

Years ago I went to a conference and the speaker called the pastors up front after the service. He and the other conference speakers laid hands on all the pastors who came forward. There were probably one hundred and fifty pastors standing across the front of the large auditorium. As these famous pastors went down the row and laid hands on the pastors, one by one, they all fell over. By the time they finished praying for everyone, I think I was the only one left standing. Now, please hear me: I wasn't resistant to receiving whatever God had for me. In fact, the whole reason I came to the conference was because I was hungry for more of God.

But I wasn't going to fake an experience to please the people praying for me, or to fit in with the crowd, or to meet anyone's expectations. I wanted an *authentic* experience with God; I didn't want to act like I had one. I wanted a real encounter with the living God—in any way He wanted to visit me. But I wasn't willing to manufacture emotions or substitute a learned behavior. I felt God's presence as I stood there, but my knees didn't buckle. I didn't sense God's weighty presence in such

> I wanted an *authentic* experience with God; I didn't want to act like I had one.

a way that it caused me to fall to the ground. I have prayed for thousands of people who have had that experience, many of whom never experienced it before. I have read about this kind of thing, again and again, in the history of revival. It happens to John in the book of Revelation and to Ezekiel multiple times in his encounters with God's glory. But I wasn't willing to pretend, and I wasn't longing for the manifestation—I was longing for God Himself.

Did every other person in line experience a powerful encounter with Jesus that caused them to fall over? Maybe. Were there some people who took a courtesy fall because they learned that was the expected behavior? (When a holy person prays for you, that's what you're supposed to do.) I don't know. Is it possible God had something for all of them and not for me? Sure. But I do know that I just wanted God for Himself, not for any particular experience or manifestation. When we substitute learned behaviors for authentic encounters, we are in danger of spiritually drifting from the source of life. We begin to substitute something learned for something real, and the problem is, if we are not careful, we will convince ourselves we have the real when all we have is a learned behavior. I don't want to find myself resisting God, nor do I want to find myself pretending to meet some expected spiritual standard. I just want the real; I want to know God Himself.

John Wesley was one of the great revivalists in history. Yet Wesley was most often rejected by the church of his day. He was unwelcomed by his own church, the Church of England. When Wesley entered a new town to preach the gospel in the open fields, there were often clergy and other people from the Anglican church who met him along the road with jeers and derision. There were even times they threw rocks at Wesley because they thought he was a heretic. These rock-throwing religious zealots who attacked the great preacher felt like they were doing a service to the church and to God, yet God was using Wesley to bring hundreds of thousands of people to know Jesus. Many Christians were revived under Wesley's ministry; entire regions were transformed by the Spirit of God through Wesley's work. Yet people resisted him and fought against him in the name of God. How did they miss what God was doing in their day?

> They had substituted the learned behaviors of religion for authentic experiences of transforming encounters with Jesus. And they didn't even know it.

I surely do not want to miss what God is doing in my day. Listen, here is the scary part: they thought they were right. They were convinced they were doing good. Like the Pharisees before them, they resisted this upstart movement in the name of God. They were passionate, zealous, and religious, but they were missing out on a real move of God. They had substituted the learned behaviors of religion for authentic experiences of transforming encounters with Jesus. And they didn't even know it. God was visiting them in one of the greatest spiritual movements in the world, and they were missing it.

God help us. I desperately want to avoid that in my life. I want to love Jesus most of all, represent Jesus well to everyone I encounter, and follow Jesus with my whole heart. I want to know Jesus personally, and not just know about Him. I want to encounter Him, experience Him, and be transformed by His presence. I want to cooperate with God to foster fresh moves of the Spirit; I don't want to find myself fighting against God. I want to avoid the pitfalls of religion and live an authentic Christian life, a life in touch with a fresh flow of the Spirit day by day. I want to be known more for Who I stand for rather than what I stand against.

I am a bit of a history buff; I love reading biographies of people who have made history. I have read over one hundred biographies of Abraham Lincoln, for example. But I don't know Abraham Lincoln. I know about him. I never had a chance to know Lincoln because he died long before I was born, so I have never been able to interact with him personally, talk with him, share my life with him, or spend time with him alone in a personal encounter. But God isn't like that, and my relationship with God can and should be much more personal than that. He doesn't just record what He is like for us in a book so we can know about Him like any other historical figure. He is alive. He speaks, He reveals Himself, and He makes Himself known to us personally. Jesus has risen and we can not only read about Him, we can encounter Him, experience Him, know Him, and hear from Him directly through the illumination of Scripture and through His direct communication. His risen presence can touch our souls, our bodies, awaken our hearts, and visit us intimately. We can actually draw near to Him, much like we can experience and know our living friends—not like we read about with a historic figure. Yes, He reveals Himself differently, but it is no less personal and no less real than a human interaction.

The problem is that it's easy to fall into all the outer trappings of a religious life without experiencing the inner workings of God. The pages of history are replete with fakers and resistors. I want to avoid both traps. I want the authentic.

Why do so many people fall into this religious ditch along their spiritual pilgrimage? We are people of routine. Most of us have a set of routines we follow every day. When I come home after driving someplace, I follow the same routine every time: I put my wallet and my keys on my dresser in my bedroom. I follow the routine so I'll know where these important items are. Doing this becomes rote, and these routines make our life easier to manage. They help us. But sometimes our routines can get us off course. For example, if I'm in a conversation with someone while driving and I'm not thinking about where I'm headed, I'll start driving on autopilot and go in the direction I travel most often. As I start toward my most common destination, Jen will say to me, "Um, we aren't going to work." In that instance my routine no longer helps me; it leads me off course.

> When my routine becomes a rut, I become religious. If I'm not careful, I may find myself reading my Bible and praying, but not going deeper with God.

Every day, one of my routines is to spend time alone with God. It's a great routine; it is a magnificent discipline to develop. I have benefited immensely from that routine, and I want to continue the habit of engaging in spiritual practices every day. That discipline has helped me know my Bible, meet with God regularly, and prepared me to encounter His presence and hear His voice. It's been an integral part of growing up in Christ and getting to know Him more personally. I don't want to lose my routine. But I do want to be aware of the dangers of this routine. I can easily put my time with God on autopilot and end up going someplace I wasn't intending to go. When my routine becomes a rut, I become religious. If I'm not careful, I may find myself reading my Bible and praying, but not going deeper with God, not becoming more like Jesus, and not maturing in love for God and people. The real problem is I may measure my maturity based on my knowledge of the Bible and my participation in these spiritual practices and not realize I am headed far from my intended destination. If I'm not careful, I may end up settling for the outer workings of religion and miss out on transformation.

Jesus said, "Not everyone who says to me, 'Lord, Lord' will enter the kingdom of heaven, but only those who do the will of my Father who is in heaven. Many will say to me on that day, 'Lord, Lord, did we not prophesy in your name and in your name drive out demons and in your name perform many miracles?' Then I will tell them plainly, 'I never knew you. Away from me, you evildoers!'" (Matthew 7:21-23) Jesus could have said that many will come on that day, saying, "Haven't we read our Bible, preached many sermons, taught many Bible studies, served at church, prayed in tongues often, and engaged in a host of other good spiritual activities?" But if all these religious activities don't lead us to love and obey God and know Him intimately, what good are they? The activities are a means to an end, not an end in themselves.

How do we develop a deep, authentic Christian life without falling prey to the religious snares? That's what I want to talk about in this book. I want to look at how we can tell when we are falling into the trap of religion. We will pay particularly close attention to the Pharisees in the gospels because they often exemplify what a religious life looks like—in all its worst aspects. They serve as a lesson and warning to us all. We will learn from them what religion looks like so we can avoid it and live a deep, intimate life with God.

We will also talk about how intimacy is developed—and not just with God but with others as well. What are the components of intimacy? What can we do to develop true intimacy with God and people so we can fulfill the first- and second-most important commandments: love God and love people? Why does our intimacy get stunted and stalled, and how can we get out of the ruts and back into the deep waters of authentic experience?

We will look at ten shifts we can make, attitudes and practices we can engage in so we can live with freshness in our relationship with God. These practices and attitudes can lead us to authentic encounters that result in deep life change and soul-satisfying intimacy. I will offer you some exercises along the way that can be helpful to developing an authentic Christian life.

We all fall prey to religion from time to time, and, periodically, every one of us needs renewal. That's one of the great lessons of church history. Sadly, as I travel the world, visit churches, and talk to Christians, I see a lot of religion. For most of these believers, it isn't that they will die and not go to Heaven. It's more that they're missing out on what could be on earth; they have settled for too little. I see a lot of religious people who need renewal. But all too often they don't realize they are religious; they have taken a wrong turn and are driving on autopilot, but they don't realize they are headed in the wrong direction. You can't get out of the trap of religion if you don't realize you are ensnared.

One of the traps of religion is that we learn all the right language. We know the right words to say, and we assume because we know the language and can speak the right words, we have the right experience. But that isn't always true. In the movement I am part of, The Christian and Missionary Alliance, historically we talked and wrote about "the deeper life." This was part of the old holiness movement and language of the deeper life. It communicated concepts of living a holy life that came out of an intimate relationship with Jesus and was empowered by the Holy Spirit. Over time people continued to speak the deeper life language, yet they missed the experiences of those who had gone before them. They talked about the deeper life, but they were living in the shallow, stagnant waters of religion. The problem is because we know the right words, and we can state the doctrines and quote the right verses to support those doctrines, sometimes we don't know we are missing the authentic. We assume knowledge means mastery, but knowledge without revelatory experience that leads to obedience only results in religion. When our knowledge isn't combined with the appropriate experiences with God, we fall into the ruts of religion. And too often we have substituted words for encounters and learned behaviors for true experiences.

Often for religious people to experience renewal, new language is going to be required. The new language creates an updated presentation of old concepts to make them new and

> Knowledge without revelatory experience that leads to obedience only results in religion.

fresh again. It helps us live an examined life. We begin to see where we are missing out, and we start to hunger for the real and authentic spiritual life. We begin to see how we have settled for less, and we begin to long for more. We need to stop, pause, evaluate our lives, and make changes that are necessary for renewal. We need to move past dusty old religion and into the deep waters of life in Christ.

One day one of our denominational leaders came to me and thanked me for writing on the deeper life. He said I had taken all the old concepts of the deeper life and put them into fresh language so a new generation could tap into the old wells of rich experience. Ultimately, my goal wasn't really to create new language for the deeper life; my goal was to create authentic experiences that led to renewal, and that required fresh language. So often religious people need to hear old concepts again, as if for the first time, so they realize there is something more. That's the nature of this journey. We have to update our language, revive our experiences, revisit our encounters, reawaken our hearts, and move from old, learned routines to fresh new experiences with the living God. That's where I want to take us in this book—from the religious to the authentic.

> So often religious people need to hear old concepts again, as if for the first time, so they realize there is something more. That's the nature of this journey.

* * * * * *

On November 27, 2023 Merriam-Webster announced its word of the year: authentic. The dictionary publishing company said it chose the word because of the rise of artificial intelligence and a spread of misinformation on social media platforms. Merriam-Webster said analytics showed a substantial increase in searches for the word in 2023, which it said was driven by stories and conversations about AI, celebrity culture, identity, and social media. Our culture is searching for the real, not the fake, not imitations. We need to be people who live an authentic Christian life so our lives are a light to a world looking for what is real. (TheHill.com published this news story about the word-of-the-year choice: https://thehill.com/blogs/in-the-know/4329748-merriam-websters-word-2023-authentic/.)

Let me end this chapter by inviting you to prepare your heart to receive all that God has for you in reading this book. One of Jesus' favorite expressions is "whoever has ears, let them hear." We need ears to hear, eyes to see, and a heart to receive what the Spirit is saying. Jesus is asking us to humble ourselves when He uses this phrase. We have to fight our base instinct to resist God; so much of our resistance is rooted in our pride. We have to fight our base instinct to conform to the cultural norms of our religious community. When we have been infected by religion, we often assume we already know that, and it limits our capacity to receive. The lens of our religion keeps us from having the eyes to see and ears to hear afresh from the Spirit. We listen and think to ourselves, *I know that*, and it inoculates us to a fresh encounter. Or we listen and immediately resist because it is outside of our experiences or comfort zone, so we assume it cannot be right or true. So let's take a moment at the beginning of this book, and let's ask the Lord to give us a humble heart, ears to hear, and eyes to see.

Lord Jesus, give us fresh revelation. We do not want to simply know about you or know the right answers. We do not want routines that lead to ruts and religion. We do not want to find ourselves resisting the next movement of God. We want to know you, to encounter you in fresh, new, and ever-deepening ways. We want to experience your tender affections, hear your voice, and walk in intimate awareness of your presence. We want to have a deep, intimate connection with you that results in us representing you well to everyone we meet, talk to, and encounter. That we would be so near to you, and you would be so real in us, that we would carry your presence to every person we encounter and, when they are with us, they would sense that they have been with you. Lord, we want to be marked by your presence because we have been with you. We want to love like you love and accept people like you accepted us while we were yet sinners. Jesus, we want you to be our first love and main obsession. So, prepare us. Give us ears to hear, eyes to see, and a heart to receive.

One

THE COUNTERFEIT

Sadly, too often I listen to Christians talk, or read what they write on their social media, and I am struck by the fact that they sound more like the Pharisees than they do like Jesus. The Pharisees represent the worst of religion in the New Testament. They are often seen battling with Jesus, judging, condemning, and stubbornly refusing to soften their hearts to Jesus' entreaties because of their absolute certainty in their righteousness and right beliefs. Yet they were people of deep commitment, and they were committed to zealous religious practices like Bible reading, praying, fasting, and tithing—applying their giving even down to the herbs in their garden. Here is the tricky part: two thousand years later, we know them as the bad guys of the story. But to the majority of the Jewish people in their day, they were the guys in the white hats who everyone looked up to, respected, and sought to emulate.

Today it is possible for us who read our Bible, pray, go to church, and do a host of other positive and accepted spiritual activities to have attitudes that more closely resemble the Pharisees than Jesus. And yet we may view ourselves as the good guys, just like the religious leaders of Jesus' day. How do we know when we are slipping into these patterns that rob us of authentic spiritual life?

Let's look closely at the Pharisees so we can see when and where this attitude of religion is creeping into our spiritual journey. I will, at times, refer to this as the "spirit" of religion. I am not specifically talking about a demonic spirit—though I will say that people who fall into these patterns of religion may have demonic spirits influencing them and even need deliverance. Mostly, I am referring to a set of beliefs, behaviors, and attitudes that are toxic to authentic spiritual depth and intimacy with God. These are the things that characterized the Pharisees who opposed Jesus and misrepresented God's heart to those they interacted with.

Let's examine six key characteristics of religion so we can break free from its clutches.

Fear

First, religion is rooted in fear. Legalism, for example, is a fear-based attempt to control people. Legalism takes the holiness standard of God and adds to it because the legalist is afraid God's standard isn't good enough. For example, God makes it clear that we should not be drunk. Drunkenness is a sin. Paul says in Ephesians 5:18, "Do not get drunk on wine, which leads to debauchery. Instead be filled with the Spirit." As Paul points out, the problem with drunkenness is that it

leads to poor choices in life. Drunk driving often leads to in-
nocent people being killed. Drunkenness sometimes causes
people to compromise their moral standard and sleep with
someone other than their spouse or to force sex upon someone who is saying no. Drunkenness (addiction) is the number
one predictor in our society that someone will grow up in a
home afflicted with domestic violence. This is why God commands us not to be drunk; God doesn't want us to get drunk
because He loves us, and He loves those around us.

With all this said, the Bible does not say that you cannot
drink. The legalist, however, is afraid that if people drink, they
will get drunk, and debauchery and horrible consequences
will result. So they state, firmly, "You cannot drink." It is a fear-
based holiness standard that one-ups the holiness standard of
God and causes us to try to control people. We don't trust people to make good decisions, so we seek to control them.

The Pharisees were notorious for laying heavy burdens
on people because of their fear-based controlling religious
standards. Jesus said of the Pharisees and teachers of the
law, "They tie up heavy, cumbersome loads and put them on
other people's shoulders, but they themselves are not willing
to lift a finger to move them" (Matthew 23:4). They used a
"catch and condemn" form of religion, not only coming out
of their own unprocessed fears, but seeking to instill fear in
others so they would be shamed into following the Pharisees'
moral standards. Matthew says, "Then the Pharisees went out
and laid plans to trap him in his words" (Matthew 22:15). The
Pharisees often laid traps for Jesus; they tried to catch him
saying something wrong so they could condemn him. This
was their approach to religion. They didn't have a sense of
self-acceptance because they were shame-based legalists, so

the only thing they had to offer others was condemnation. They saw Jesus as a threat to their power and control, so they tried to catch him doing things that were wrong so they could condemn him before all the people.

Romans 8:1 tells us, "Therefore, there is now no condemnation for those who are in Christ Jesus." Jesus said, "For God did not send his Son into the world to condemn the world, but to save the world through him" (John 3:17). Jesus' purpose in coming was to release us from condemnation. He doesn't have any condemnation or judgment to offer; He has come into the world to save us from sin, judgment, and condemnation. His arms are open to anyone who will humbly come to Him. This catch-and-condemn attitude of the Pharisees is not the heart of Jesus. It is the spirit of religion. Jesus wasn't focused on pointing out everyone's wrongdoing; He came to offer people a path to forgiveness and hope. He came to display God's love.

> This catch-and-condemn attitude is not the heart of Jesus. It is the spirit of religion.

Often when we are infected by the spirit of religion, we struggle to feel accepted before God. We wrestle with shame. Shame makes us feel like we aren't good enough; if people knew us, they would not accept us. We are broken, damaged, unlovable, and irreparable. When we feel shame, we usually tend to be hard on ourselves, hard on others, or both. The next time you find yourself being hard on yourself or feeling like you need to crawl across glass to come back to God after falling into a besetting sin, recognize that you are acting on fear: the fear that you aren't good enough to be accepted in Christ. Paul said, "The Spirit you received does not make you slaves so you live in fear again; rather, the Spirit you received brought about your adoption to sonship" (Romans 8:15). You have been adopted in Christ and have firstborn son status—you are an heir of God and a coheir with Christ (Romans 8:17). Don't let the enemy reduce you into religious slavery again.

Our judgment of others most often comes out of our unprocessed wounds. Our judgments reveal more about us than they do about others. We judge others because we haven't come to peace with God and ourselves through Jesus' death. We know that we are forgiven, but we still don't feel forgiven. We know that we are loved, but we don't feel loved. We know we are accepted, but we are still striving to gain God's approval. We have hurts and wounds that are festering within us, and when someone bumps up against us, we judge them through the unprocessed pain in our soul. The problem is that often we are so used to the pain that it has become normal to us, and we do not realize it is tainting our judgments. The next time you catch yourself thinking negatively and critically about another person, ask yourself: *Where is that coming from? What unprocessed wound of mine may have led me to these negative judgments?*

Fear also makes us self-centered. The Pharisees were consumed with themselves. They felt threatened by Jesus because of His growing success and fruitfulness. They were afraid that Jesus' growing popularity would diminish their importance in the eyes of people. They loved the applause of the people, but now Jesus was attracting the crowds. Even Pilate recognized that it was because of envy that they wanted to kill Jesus (Matthew 27:18). Our envy of others comes out of our own fear—fear that someone else will surpass us in success, in recognition, in love. Our fear causes us to be self-focused and lose our way.

Fear gets us focused on minutia and causes us to miss the big picture. The Pharisees were focused on the little things. Jesus said to them, "Woe to you, teachers of the law and Pharisees, you hypocrites! You give a tenth of your spices—mint, dill, and cumin. But you have neglected the more important matters of the law—justice, mercy, and faithfulness. You should have practiced the latter, without neglecting the former. You blind guides! You strain out a gnat but swallow a camel" (Matthew 23:23, 24). When we become religious, our fear-based approach to life and God causes us to miss the big picture and obsess about the wrong things. We dig in our heels on secondary issues. We die on the wrong hills, but we don't know we are doing it. We make a living attacking others for what they do wrong or for their wrong beliefs, and we become more known for what we stand against than for who we stand for. We feel we are in the right because we are unwilling to humble ourselves and admit when we are in the wrong. We feel threatened, irritated, and aggravated by people's behaviors and beliefs, and we don't really know why; we just assume it's because we are right and they are wrong. But Jesus wasn't that way; the Pharisees were.

> Jesus was loving to those who lived sinfully, and the Pharisees couldn't stand for His perceived moral compromise.

Jesus was loving to those who lived sinfully, and the Pharisees couldn't stand for His perceived moral compromise.

Jesus said the main thing is to love God and love people. Yet some people, in their fear, are seeking to guard their version of the truth, but in their effort to hold onto the truth let go of love. I've had people attack me because they claim I am a false teacher over the subject of deliverance ministries. If we sat down and could have a reasonable discussion, we would likely agree on every single major doctrinal issue: who Jesus is, the doctrine of the Trinity, the inspiration of the Scriptures, salvation through faith in Jesus and His work on the cross only, and so on. Yet they cannot allow themselves to have an honorable and loving conversation with someone who disagrees with them on certain secondary doctrinal themes. Often our fear causes us to lose the big picture, lose sight of the most important things, and become ungracious, all in the name of God, over smaller doctrinal issues that do not take up much space in the New Testament. That's religion.

Religious people struggle with a core of fear. They are motivated by fear. Fear is a powerful and primal emotion, so when it gets stirred up, we often become heated, angry, defensive, and lose our way. Often at Soul Care Conferences during a question-and-answer time, I will remark to a person that their question is motivated by fear. People will ask me, for example: "How do you protect yourself from the enemy when you are doing all these conferences and all these deliverances?" Or "What if you're doing deliverance and a spirit jumps on you?" Or "If we are doing deliverance, will a demon leave a person and enter us or our children?" Do you hear the fear in those questions? Do you think Jesus ever asked himself any of those questions? Do you think Jesus wandered around and fearfully thought: How will I protect myself from all the demonic attacks because I am doing deliverance ministries? Will the demons jump on me? Will they attack my mother? Jesus never asked himself questions like these because they are rooted in

> Here is a key principle to remember: *When we ask ourselves a question that Jesus never would have asked himself, that is most often a fear-based religious question.*

fear. Here is a key principle to remember: *When we ask ourselves a question that Jesus never would have asked himself, that is most often a fear-based religious question.* If we are going to break free from religion, we have to recognize how often we are motivated by fear. If we fail to recognize it, we are in bondage to it.

If you are beginning to see that you have some fear motivating you, then you have to frequently stop and ask yourself: Is this thought, question, action, desire, or emotional reaction motivated by fear? Would Jesus think this way or act this way? Be honest, and don't let fear rule your life—it will always make you religious.

If we have read our Bible or gone to church for a while, we know the solution to overcoming fear. Many of us have even memorized this verse: "There is no fear in love. But perfect love drives out fear" (1 John 4:18). But if you quote the verse, and don't overcome the fear, that's just religion. If you quote the verse, but don't live it out, you are missing out on the freedom Jesus has made available to you. Knowledge without transformation leads to religion. You are substituting your knowledge of the truth for authentic, victorious Christian living. So it's not enough to know it; you have to live it. The verse goes on to say: "The one who fears is not made perfect in love" (1 John 4:18). If we are still wrestling with fear-based questions, fear-based motives, and fear-based actions, it's because love has not been perfected in us. We have the right words, we know the right verses, but we haven't figured out how to live out our faith so that we're experiencing Christ's victories. And that is the very nature of religion: what we know hasn't made its way into our *living*. We have to live it, not just declare it, quote it, and talk about it. Earlier in the text John said, "And so we know and rely on the love God has for us" (1 John 4:16). See, it isn't enough to know it, we must learn how to rely upon God's love in such a way that it drives out fear. That is when we have moved from religion to authentic experience.

In my books *Soul Care, Spiritual Authority,* and *The Soul Care Leader*, I talk about how I learned to rely on the love of God. There is more information there if you need a breakthrough in this area. But the short version is I learned to hold onto the truth of God's love by renewing my mind with the truth, in Scripture, about who I am in Christ, and by listening to the Spirit's testimony that I am deeply loved by God (Romans 8:14). I learned to live like a deeply loved person by relying on God's love day by day.

I had a fear of not being loved that caused me to wall up with silence in my early years of marriage. I would have a desire or expectation or goal that Jen wasn't meeting, and I would feel hurt, and I would choose silence. It was a wall of self-protection, and it was manipulative, and I had to get to the place where I learned to rely on God's love and give up my silence. I didn't give myself permission to continue to act in these silent, manipulative ways. I apologized to Jen, asked her forgiveness, and gave her permission to call me on it if I did it again. And I learned to rely on God's love.

When I could feel the silent walls coming up within my soul, instead of acting on those emotions, I went to Jesus. I sat in His presence. I renewed my mind and listened to the Spirit testify that He loved me. Then I asked myself and God: "How would a deeply loved person act?" I submitted myself to God and did what He asked: I went and had a direct and honest conversation with Jen without resorting to silence. I learned how to ask her directly for what I wanted, without demanding that she do it, or punishing her with silence if she didn't do it. Day by day I learned to rely on God's love, and it drove out that fear of not being loved.

Too often in the church we ask the wrong question. We ask people, "Do you know you are loved by God?" If people have read their Bible and gone to church, they will know the right answer. But it's the wrong question. The right question is: *Are you living like a deeply loved person in all your human interactions?* That's when you have broken free from fear and are living out your faith in an authentic way. If you are still defensive, passive-aggressive, and insecure, then you know you are loved by God, but you aren't living like a deeply loved person. Lots of people know they are loved by God and yet live like unloved people—they are insecure, full of self-doubt, defensive, slow to apologize, slow to admit wrongs, always have to be right, are anxious, easily offended, or some combination, or many, of the above. James says, "Faith without deeds is dead." If you know you are loved by God, but you're living like an unloved person, your faith is dead to you; it isn't making any difference in your freedom and fullness in life. We have to integrate the love of God into our daily existence so we live like deeply loved people. That's authentic faith!

Sadly, Christians are often the most fear-based people I know, and this is utterly unbecoming a son or daughter of the King.

Sadly, Christians are often the most fear-based people I know, and this is utterly unbecoming a son or daughter of the King. We can overcome in Christ. How big a role does fear play in your life? Where is fear motivating you? Are you living under judgment or condemnation because of fear? Are you living like a deeply loved person? Has love been perfected in your life sufficiently to drive out fear-based responses to life's unwelcome circumstances?

Pride

Second, religion is characterized by pride. The Pharisees were too proud to examine their faulty worldview, and that led them to miss who Jesus was. They were too proud to admit when they were wrong and too proud to learn from Jesus or others. If you are only open to learn from those you already agree with, you aren't learning much.

We often become proud in our religious practices; we take pride in our devotional lifestyle of Bible reading, prayer, church attendance, and service, just like the Pharisees did. They loved public prayer and the admiration of people. Jesus said of them, "Everything they do is done for people to see: They make their phylacteries wide and the tassels on their garments long; they love the place of honor at banquets and the most important seats in the synagogues; they love to be greeted with respect in the marketplaces and to have people call them 'Rabbi'" (Matthew 23:5-7). But if we take pride in our religious practices, we will inevitably lose our way on the journey to intimacy with God, because God opposes the proud. These practices will become an end in themselves, not a means to an end. They will become a measure of our maturity, not an aide to our maturity. They will become a means to be seen as spiritual rather than to develop true depth with God. The purpose of reading your Bible is not to know the Bible; the purpose of reading your Bible is to encounter the living God. God gave us the Bible so we could know Him personally, not know about Him.

> The purpose of reading your Bible is not to know the Bible; the purpose of reading your Bible is to encounter the living God.

When you get to Heaven there won't be any need for a Bible because you will have God Himself. If we read our Bible without encountering God, we will likely grow proud of our disciplines and our Bible knowledge, and yet grow distant from God because of our pride.

The Pharisees complained to Jesus that the disciples were not following the traditions of the elders; they weren't ceremonially washing their hands properly before they ate, the Pharisees protested. Jesus pointed out how they twisted the intent of the law for their own purposes. And then he quoted Isaiah and applied it to them when he said, "You hypocrites! Isaiah was right when he prophesied about you: 'These people honor me with their lips, but their hearts are far from me. They worship me in vain'" (Matthew 15:7-9). It is far too easy to allow our religious practices to become a scorecard to measure our maturity rather than a compass to lead us to encountering God Himself. Sometimes the result is that we read our Bible and pray because that's what good Christians do, but we aren't encountering God in the text; we are gaining knowledge and improving our opinion of ourselves as spiritual people.

Again, too often we ask the wrong question. We ask someone, "Are you spending time with God?" The right question: "Is your spiritual rhythm working?" Your rhythm is what you do on a daily, weekly, monthly, and yearly basis to grow in intimacy with God and in Christlike maturity. Are your practices of Bible reading, prayer, fasting, service, and the like producing spiritual maturity? Are you becoming more loving? Do you love God and love people more this year than you did last year? If not, you may be doing the right things, but you may be growing more religious in the process. Jesus said the first and most important law is love. So be honest: are you becoming more loving? Would the people around you tell you that you are? Ask them, and don't defend yourself if they don't think so! Do you feel peace and joy? The fruit of the Spirit begins with love, joy, and peace. So, are your spiritual efforts making you experience more love, joy, and peace? Are you experiencing more of God's presence, hearing his voice more clearly and frequently in your life? Jesus said that His sheep would hear His voice (John 10:27). Are you representing Jesus well to those around you? When they are with you, do they love Him more?

When we are more concerned with being right than we are with being in right relationship, then our spiritual journey is amiss. When we are more argumentative than we are loving, our spiritual practices aren't truly helpful. I was a part of a Bible study when I was in my twenties. It was a multigenerational, multidenominational group that was truly enriching. The group was great for me spiritually and relationally in the year between college and seminary. After my first year of seminary, I went back to the group to visit my friends. We ended up in a theological debate over Calvinism versus Arminianism. No one was disrespectful, but after the debate, after everyone else had gone home, the leader of the group very gently and graciously spoke to me. He said that he felt I had lost some of my passion for Jesus in my zeal to gain knowledge. I had become more theologically astute, but less on fire for God. I was getting caught up in the learning, and my theological opinions, and I was missing the big picture. I went home and repented. The most important things are to love Jesus and love people. If all our learning doesn't make us more loving, something is seriously off in our souls, and we are becoming more like the Pharisees and less like Jesus.

A.W. Tozer, in his book *The Pursuit of God,* wrote, "The world is perishing for lack of the knowledge of God, and the church is famishing for want of His Presence. The instant cure of most of our religious ills would be to enter the Presence in spiritual experience, to become suddenly aware that we are in God and God is in us. This would lift us out of our pitiful narrowness and cause our hearts to be enlarged" (Tozer, *The Pursuit of God,* Christian Publications, Camp Hill, 1993, p. 36).

We need to have more than knowledge if we are going to become people of true depth; we must have encounters with the living Christ that lead us to Christlike transformation. Paul said, "Knowledge puffs up while love builds up" (1 Corinthians 8:1). When we encounter Jesus, we are changed by His love, and we become like Him. When we grow in knowledge without encountering Jesus, we become proud and all too often misrepresent Jesus to those around us.

Speaking of the early church fathers and their shaping encounters with God, Tozer wrote: "They habitually spoke with spiritual authority. They had been in the presence of God and they reported what they saw there. They were prophets, not scribes, for the scribe tells us what he has read, and the prophet tells us what he has seen. The distinction is not an imaginary one . . . we are overrun today with orthodox scribes, but the prophets, where are they? The hard voice of the scribe sounds over evangelicalism, but the church waits for the tender voice of the saint who has penetrated the veil and has gazed with inward eye upon the wonder that is God. And yet, thus to penetrate to push in sensitive living experience into the Holy Presence, is a privilege open to every child of God" (Tozer, *The Pursuit of God*, p. 40).

How can we represent Jesus well if we haven't encountered Him but only know about Him? How can our flame burn hot for Jesus unless we are encountering His holy presence? We may burn hot for our theological opinions, our biblical interpretations, and our ministerial contributions, but that is not the same as burning hot for Jesus. My greatest passion in life is to love Jesus and represent Him well to everyone I encounter. I need to know Him to do that, not know about Him. It is in my encounters with Jesus that I have been transformed. I can't represent Jesus well without being marked by His presence. It is in my experiences with Jesus that I have fallen in love with Him more and more.

> My greatest passion in life is to love Jesus and represent Him well to everyone I encounter. I need to know Him to do that, not know about Him.

If we are going to break free from religion, we must develop authentic humility. God is irresistibly attracted to the contrite of heart, but the proud walk alone. Authentic humility begins with honesty, ends with responsibility, and somewhere in the middle is death to self. When we die to self, we stop making it all about us, and we make it all about Jesus. Proud people cannot admit they are wrong. They spin, defend, blame, justify, and deny. Proud people are too wrapped up in their own opinions and feel the need to prove they are right. Often this is rooted in shame and insecurity, but shame is merely pride wrapped in self-disgust. Shame, pride, and insecurity all make life too much about us. It is not easy to admit wrongdoing. It is difficult to humble ourselves; it goes against our sinful nature.

In the early years of marriage, when Jen and I hit our biggest marriage snag, one of the primary things that was preventing us from moving forward was our inability to humble ourselves and admit wrongdoing. I kept defending myself. One day the Lord spoke to me in my inner being and said, "Only insecure people defend themselves. Every time you defend yourself you are deflecting the truth I offer to help you grow." I had to learn how to cultivate humility and own my part. I had to resist my feelings of defensiveness and die to self, and instead listen and learn to take ownership for my wrongs.

The good news is that I have grown. My daughter Darcy called me one day and said, "Dad, I got angry with the child I was babysitting today. I called him over and held him in my arms and apologized to him. We cried together." Then she paused and said, "I learned that from you, Dad. You never did something wrong as a parent except I remember you apologizing for it." I think the two most important things you can do as a parent are, first, to demonstrate love and communicate love to your children; second, to apologize when you blow it.

Now, I wish I could tell you I have reached the point where I don't feel defensive anymore, but sadly, that is not true. Recently, someone attacked me on a public platform, and my immediate reaction was anger and defensiveness. I vented for a few minutes to Jen. Then I apologized to her, got back on the true foundation of Jesus' love for me, blessed those who cursed me, and let it go. It took me ten minutes to get past it. I would love to get to the place where I am humble enough that I feel no anger, defensiveness, or angst when I am criticized, but I am not there yet. I long for that day. In the meantime, I try not to respond in the moment. I don't counterattack, I don't defend myself; I do my best to avoid all imaginary conversations with the person in my head. I process it with Jesus and get back to living off my identity in Christ as a deeply loved child of God.

> That is the way of the authentic spiritual journey. We love God more, we love people more, and we make life less about us.

I'm not the man I want to be, but I'm not the man I used to be either. I used to stew over these sorts of things for days, holding imaginary conversations with the person in my head. Now, most of the time, I can get past them in a matter of minutes. I am making definite progress making life less about me. That is the way of the authentic spiritual journey. We love God more, we love people more, and we make life less about us.

Control

Third, religion is characterized by control. Jesus was empowering. He empowered people to make choices. For instance, He let the rich young ruler walk away; He loved the wealthy man as he chose wealth over Jesus. He empowered His disciples to do ministry even though He was clearly better at it than they were, and they were still constantly making it too much about themselves. He gave them authority to preach the gospel of the kingdom, cast out demons, and heal the sick. Jesus gave up His heavenly throne and became a child. Paul writes, "In your relationships with one another, have the same attitude of mind Christ Jesus had: 'Who, being in very nature God, did not consider equality with God something to be used for his own advantage; rather, he made himself nothing by taking the very nature of a servant, being made in human likeness'" (Philippians 2:5-7). Jesus did not clutch to His power as a member of the Trinity. He was willing to set aside His rights to utilize His divine attributes. When He was here on planet earth He operated fully as a human in dependence on the Father—just as we must. He limited Himself to one place at a time, giving up His right to His omnipresence. He was, instead, totally dependent on the Father for supernatural power. He never ceased to be divine, but He gave up His rights to use His divine attributes while on the earth. He did not clutch to His divinity and insist upon His rights.

> He never ceased to be divine, but He gave up His rights to use His divine attributes while on the earth.

Yet when we are falling into the traps of religion, we don't act like Jesus did. We fight for our rights. The Pharisees fought for their position, power, and honor. They fought for their reputation and recognition. John 11:47, 48 says, "Then the chief priests and the Pharisees called a meeting of the Sanhedrin. 'What are we accomplishing?' they asked. 'Here is this man performing many signs. If we let him go on like this, everyone will believe in him.'"

They didn't care that Jesus was performing miraculous signs that were benefitting people; they didn't ask how it could be possible that He was performing signs and wonders. They didn't wonder how it could be that the eyes of those born blind were opened, or how it was that the demonized were delivered with a word, or that people were raised from the dead by Jesus. They didn't stop to examine that they may have been wrong in their opinions about Jesus. Pride made them married to their opinions and caused them to take control of the situation in evil ways. They were only consumed with the reality that everyone was going to believe in Him—and that had to be stopped at any cost. God help us. When we live religious lives without surrendered hearts we will inevitably opt for human forms of power and control. We will be easily threatened by people who disagree with our opinions, and we will seek to persuade them to our positions and/or criticize them when we can't win them over. We will be liable to become agitated, aggravated, and angry with godly people who hold differing theological views from our own.

During COVID there were all sorts of battles taking place in the church over inconsequential matters that became primary obsessions: masks or no masks, vaccines or no vaccines. We were, too often, obsessed with our rights and our opinions, but too seldom obsessed with Jesus and motivated by love. And inevitably, when we become obsessed with our opinions and rights, we are moved to fight for control. It ended up causing lots of divisions in the church. Many people left their church, and many others quit going to church altogether. And perhaps most sadly of all, many nonbelievers who may have been persuaded to come to church and find Jesus were repelled by the infighting in the church. All because people were more concerned with their rights, their opinions, and getting their way rather than with Jesus and His kingdom. That's religion. When I hear Christians fighting for their rights, I often say, "When you decided to follow Jesus, you gave up your rights. The only right you have left is the right to take up your cross and die." It's not very American of me, it's not very popular, but it is the call of Jesus on our lives. When we are more American than we are Christian, we are more religious than we are Christlike. When we are more infatuated with our opinions and our rights than we are obsessed with Jesus and His kingdom, we have lost our way. And if we want an authentic spiritual depth, there is no path to arrive there that does not include the cross. Any way that is focused more on self than the cross is a counterfeit way, not the authentic way of Jesus.

> If we want an authentic spiritual depth, there is no path to arrive there that does not include the cross.

Sometimes control manifests in our religious practices as a form of self-reserve, extreme caution, and/or shutting down certain expressions or manifestations because we deem them false or they make us uncomfortable. When people broke out in praise as Jesus came into Jerusalem on what we call Palm Sunday, the Pharisees told Jesus to rebuke His disciples. They didn't want these loud, exuberant outbursts of praise, especially as they were directed toward Jesus' arrival (Luke 19:39, 40). Yet Jesus would not tell them to stop. Instead, He said that if they stopped, the rocks would cry out in songs of praise.

In the early days of the First Great Awakening, there were times when John Wesley sent the crowds home because of the loud manifestations that were taking place. People in the crowd were often wailing in repentance while others broke into gales of laughter because they were touched by God's loving presence. Wesley was uncomfortable with all the emotional displays and many of the spiritual manifestations that were occurring. They were outside his normal church experience. So, at times, he would tell everyone to go home and come back the next day. But eventually Wesley realized that if he continued to shut everything down, he would quench the Holy Spirit, so he chose to let things take place that were beyond his comfort zone.

My friend Ron Walborn has observed that often what we call discernment is merely our comfort zone. If it isn't something we are used to, something we have experienced, then we want to shut it down. We want to control it because it makes us uncomfortable. We say it isn't from God—but the reality may be that we are just uncomfortable because it is outside the realm of our current experience. If our comfort zone limits what we consider acceptable in the kingdom, we will never see anything beyond what we have already seen.

I was talking to a group of Evangelicals years ago, at about the time the Toronto Airport revival first broke out, and this group was mocking holy laughter and saying that what was happening in Toronto wasn't from God because holy laughter isn't from God. There were probably twenty or more people in the group, but I decided to venture onto thin ice. I said, "Do you think the First Great Awakening under John Wesley's leadership was a legitimate revival?" They all thought it was. I told them that Wesley records in his journal the phenomena of holy laughter taking place, though he doesn't call it by that name. I asked if they thought the revival under Charles Finney, known as the Second Great Awakening, was legitimate. They were a little more circumspect but admitted they thought it was. I told them that Finney too described holy laughter taking place in the public revival meetings, though once again he didn't use that phrase to describe it. The first time the term *holy laughter* appears in history, as far as I can trace it, is by John Praying Hyde, an American missionary to India. Hyde described the same phenomena and named it holy laughter. It has occurred frequently throughout the pages of history, especially during times of revival. Just because we don't feel comfortable with something doesn't mean it is not from God. Just because we ourselves have never experienced it doesn't mean that someone else's experience is not legitimate. I personally have not experienced holy laughter, but I have prayed for people who have and can tell that it is the Holy Spirit touching them in a very deep way. Our fear and pride may cause us to control things and shut things down that God is initiating. We must be careful or we will find ourselves resisting God because of our religiosity, just like the Pharisees.

Sometimes control manifests as attacks on other people. We criticize and condemn those who disagree with us and may even villainize them by calling them false teachers. The false teacher label, in the New Testament, seems to be reserved for those who, first of all, preach a different gospel; that is, they are teaching another path to salvation other than repentance and faith in Jesus Christ (e.g., Galatians 1:6-9). Or secondly, for those who teach something not true about the Godhead, like denying that Jesus came in the flesh or denying that He is God. Or third, they live an unholy life and are doing their ministry out of spurious motives and may not even be following Jesus at all (for example, Matthew 7:15-23). I have been called a false teacher for my teaching on deliverance which, even if I am wrong, isn't false teaching. I think those who oppose deliverance are wrong—but I wouldn't call them false teachers. I simply disagree with them. I have both biblical and experiential reasons to believe that I am right, and I would bet my house on it, but I still wouldn't call those who disagree with me false teachers.

I disagree with many people theologically on all sorts of issues that would not disqualify us from fellowship nor cause me to label them as false teachers. I believe that all the gifts of the Spirit are operative, and that miracles happen today. I have seen many miracles. But I wouldn't call someone who doesn't believe in miracles a false teacher. I believe they are mistaken, I believe they are wrong, I believe that their Western worldview has impaired their biblical lenses. But I still would not call them false teachers. When we start going after people's hearts, their character, and labeling them as false teachers for a secondary doctrinal point, that is religion. That is the method of the Pharisees.

This form of control leads to attacks and divisiveness that misrepresent Jesus. It causes us to judge others who love Jesus with all their heart. But Paul said, "Who are you to judge someone else's servant? To their own master they stand or fall.

And they will stand, for the Lord is able to make them stand" (Romans 14:4). The problem is when we feel threatened by the differing viewpoints of others because of our own insecurities, we judge and attack those who disagree. That is the spirit of religion. We need to learn to be humble enough to agree to disagree on secondary matters without falling into the religious path of villainizing those we disagree with, and certainly not attacking those for whom Christ died.

Sadly, sometimes we judge people who disagree with us without even listening to them ourselves. We base our judgment on someone else's opinion of them. Recently, I was at a conference and someone told me they had a friend leave the church that hosted the conference because they asked another pastor about *Soul Care*. They hadn't read the book themselves; they merely judged me and judged *Soul Care* based on someone else's opinion. We need to have more wisdom than this in life or we will find ourselves opposing Jesus.

Often what motivates these attacks is envy. Someone is jealous and/or envious of another person for something they have or something they did or something they are, and they resort to tearing another person down to feel better about themselves. The Pharisees did this with Jesus, and eventually they crucified Him. I once met with a man who was angry with me, veins popping out of his neck, spitting-wrath angry. He was attacking me publicly and his attacks were always cloaked in religious arguments and rooted in theological objections. According to him, I was compromising the truth; I was a false teacher. But he had signed a doctrinal statement that agreed with the same things I was teaching. One day I sat with the Lord and asked, "Why? Why is this man so angry with me?" I heard the Lord say, "He is envious." I asked, "Why? What does he have to envy me about?" The Lord told me it was because of my relationship with his wife. She had done nothing wrong and had always been pure and appropriate with me. But I later discovered that she had an emotional attachment to me, and that led the man to his angry, jealous, irrational response. Unfortunately, rather than dealing with his insecurities, talking to me honestly, or processing his own issues privately with God, he resorted to angry attacks and chose to damage Jesus' bride in the name of his religious fervor. Make no mistake about it: that is the way of the Pharisees. It is the spirit of religion, but it is not the way of Jesus.

In the name of Jesus, please don't be like that. Don't damage the church because of your insecurity and pride that results in jealousy and control. Be honest about your motives; be humble and repent of your pride and put the cause of Christ before yourself. The problem is that envy is such an insidious emotion. We feel this jealous envy and start to look where the other person is wrong, we question their motives, pick on their character flaws, nitpick their beliefs, and spiritualize our evil intentions just like the Pharisees did with Jesus. We justify our envious motives and vilify our enemy's beliefs so we can sanctify our divisive behaviors. There is a lot of this going on in the church today, and it is unbecoming of us as Christ-followers and damaging our mission.

Someone I know wrote a book, and I found myself wishing he would do well, just not as well as I did. I could have looked at some of the things he wrote that I disagreed with and tried to justify my thinking based on theological differences, but that would have been disingenuous. It is sadly and simply pride and envy, so I confessed it to the Lord, repented of it, and prayed that the person's book would be used greatly by God. I didn't attack the book and talk about the person's wrong thinking, poor theology, or label it as false teaching. I dealt with my sinful heart before the Lord. I don't want to be that kind of small-hearted, small-minded, self-focused person; I want to be a person who roots for the Kingdom of God to advance over my own cause. You must battle your bias toward self with honest confession and the way of the cross.

> You must battle your bias toward self with honest confession and the way of the cross.

Tragically, I realize that most of the people who have taken to attacking other Christians are not going to read this and repent, so I am mostly writing to those of you who are influenced by them. Please, don't fall prey to this kind of thinking.

Man-Made Solutions

Fourth, religion is characterized by man-made solutions to God-sized problems. Religious people are often threatened by the power of God. It opposes their control issues, and if someone experiences power and they don't, then they either have to repent of their powerless theology and experience or they need to find fault with the person moving in power. That's what the religious leaders did with Jesus. They accused Him of casting out demons by the power of Beelzebul (Luke 11:15). They saw Him do miracles and deliverances, so they had to find some way to explain them away, or else give Him credit—they chose to claim that Jesus worked by the power of the devil. In Matthew 22:29 Jesus said to the Sadducees, another group of religious leaders who did not believe in the resurrection, "You are in error because you do not know the Scriptures or the power of God." That's a powerful statement. These are people who have saturated their lives in the study of the Scriptures, and yet Jesus said that they didn't know the Scriptures. They had a powerless theology that was not at all rooted in biblical reality; it was rooted in their impoverished experience. We often create theology out of our experience or lack thereof, and when someone else has a different experience that leads to a different theology (especially power), we demonize them—they are doing it by the power of the devil or they are a false teacher. I once literally had someone accuse me of casting out demons by the power of Beelzebul. It was one of the most complimentary attacks I've ever received!

In some Evangelical churches these man-made solutions show up as a fear of the Holy Spirit. Please listen: Jesus isn't afraid of the Holy Spirit; fear of the Holy Spirit is demonic. It is a tool of the enemy to keep us from freedom and fullness in Christ. Paul said that in the last days there would be people "having a form of godliness but denying its power" (2 Timothy 3:5). Like the Pharisees and Sadducees, they would be religious people threatened by the power of God. They would be comfortable with things they can control, things they can understand with human reason, but would attack things that are mysterious and supernatural. And yet, God is supernatural. This is a supernatural life we are called to live: a major premise of the New Testament is that we are in Christ and Christ is in us. There is a mystical, supernatural union taking place that allows us to have intimacy with a God who is invisible yet within us who believe. He communes with us, empowers us, and manifests Himself to us. It is this supernatural union that allows us to live a supernaturally empowered life. Being afraid of the Spirit is a demonic tool to keep us from experiencing the supernatural life available in Christ. So we tighten controls, we emphasize the Bible over the Spirit rather than the Bible *and* the Spirit, and we honor skepticism over faith. But there is no honor for the skeptic in the New Testament; the honor is always reserved for the faith-filled person. This is religion: it is a form of godliness denying its power.

> This is religion: it is a form of godliness denying its power.

In some Pentecostal churches we substitute learned behaviors for authentic experiences. For example, as a guest speaker sometimes I will pray with people after a service in Pentecostal or Charismatic churches, and sometimes the person will take a courtesy fall. They have learned that when a holy person prays for you, you are supposed to fall over; that has become culturally normal to them. Let me say two things about this: first, this does happen, and it is real. I have prayed for thousands of people over the years who have fallen because the presence of God became so heavy during our prayer time that they could no longer stand. Wesley and Finney both describe this happening in the First and Second Great Awakenings. In my own tribe, the Christian and Missionary Alliance, in our early history they spoke of "prostrations"— people falling over in the presence of the Lord. It happened to John the Apostle in Revelation when he encountered the risen Christ; he fell over like a dead man (which is where, I think, the phrase "slain in the Spirit" originated from). It happened to Ezekiel multiple times in the Old Testament when he encountered the glory of God. So I believe in this phenomenon and have seen it over and over. But the second thing I want to say is that sometimes people fall over not because the power of God comes upon them, but because they know it is what they are supposed to do. They don't want to be perceived as less spiritual, so they fall on cue. This is a learned behavior, and the person is substituting learned behaviors for authentic experience. That's religion, and it is a man-made solution to spiritual reality.

Whether we resist the power of God, like the religious leaders, because our theology doesn't make space for it, or we try to manufacture the manifestations of God's power by faking it—either way, that is religion. We should seek God for Himself and neither resist nor manufacture the manifestations of the Spirit. We don't need the manifestation; we need God. We don't need to be afraid of the Holy Spirit, nor do we need to imitate the accepted practices of our religious group to please people and fake a religious experience to look spiritual. Rather, let's choose this path: seek God, not the manifestations, and let the manifestations come as God wills, without fear.

Often, man-made solutions litter our path to salvation and sanctification. The Pharisees, and many groups since, have tried to make salvation about works. You have to be good enough, do enough good deeds, and try harder in order to earn favor with God. Others, who have claimed salvation by grace through faith, lay heavy burdens on people for sanctification—they go beyond God's holiness standards with legalistic requirements. These are man-made solutions that are typical of religion. With religion there often is a checklist mentality. We have a checklist for spiritual maturity; typically, we have a list of things we must do to be mature, and a list of things we can't do. We must read our Bible, pray, go to church, tithe, serve, evangelize, and so on. We can't lust, can't be angry, can't be greedy, can't drink, can't smoke, and can't dance if we are going to be acceptable to God. (These are just examples, of course; the lists may vary.)

These become the marks of maturity: "good Christians do this; they don't do that." Of course, when we don't live up to these standards, it feeds our shame, and if we are living up to them, it feeds our pride. Both pride and shame make life too much about us and rob us of our attention on and affection for Jesus. This leads me to my next point about the counterfeit.

Performance

Fifth, religion emphasizes our performance. Jesus said that the teachers of the law "tie up heavy, cumbersome loads and put them on other people's shoulders, but they themselves are not willing to lift a finger to move them" (Matthew 23:4). In His famous parable of the Pharisee and the tax collector, Jesus said, "The Pharisee stood by himself and prayed: 'God, I thank you that I am not like other people—robbers, evildoers, adulterers—or even like this tax collector. I fast twice a week and give a tenth of all I get'" (Luke 19:11, 12). The Pharisee measures how good he is by comparing himself to others. He measures his spiritual maturity

> Religion emphasizes our performance. Jesus said that the teachers of the law "tie up heavy, cumbersome loads and put them on other people's shoulders."

by his spiritual disciplines, his better behavior than others, and his dutiful obedience. But sadly, without even knowing it, he has missed the heart of God. He has missed the main thing—loving God and loving people. He sits in self-righteous self-evaluation and stands in judgment of others.

Too often, like this Pharisee, when we fall prey to religion, we are known more for what we stand against than for Who we stand for. We are known for hating things—sexual immorality, sexual perversion, abortion, and a host of other things. But we are not known for our great love for God and others. Yet when you read the gospels the thing that Jesus is most known for, and most attacked for, is His love for sinners. The Pharisees are known for their distaste for sinners. How is it that too often we have become more like the Pharisees than like Jesus? The answer is that we have fallen into religiosity. We have substituted learned behaviors for authentic encounters; we have traded "correct beliefs" for a contrite heart; we have measured maturity by outer standards rather than inner motivations. We are looking at the outside of the dish, not the inside, as Jesus told the Pharisees.

One of the problems with this performance-based approach to religion is that it often leads to legalism, which we talked about earlier. All this legalism leaves us with shame and pride that results in the judgment of others. We look at other people who don't live up to our standards, and we are repulsed. They seem vile to us, but we fail to realize this is because of the pride we take in our religious standards of righteousness. When we take pride in our righteousness, it always becomes self-righteousness, which always leads to judgment of others. I believe God's standard for sexuality is one man, one woman in a marriage covenant for life. That is how I have lived my life.

I was traveling recently, and I went to a restaurant by myself, which happens a lot when I am on the road. There was no place to sit, so I sat and ate at the bar. There were two guys next to me at the bar; they were probably both in their forties and were talking about picking up girls. I wasn't repulsed or reviled by what I was listening to, but I have to confess, I felt sad for them. I felt grieved that this is their life, that they are missing out on something better God has for them, and they don't know it. I also felt grateful that I have Jen, and that we have been married since 1990 and have figured out how to have a deep and meaningful relationship. When I see someone who is transgender or gay or a serial adulterer or promiscuous, I don't want to judge them. That was the way of the Pharisees, but it wasn't the way of Jesus. I want to simply love them because that's how Jesus was, even with people who didn't live up to God's moral standards. This is a matter of the condition of the heart. If I take pride in my performance, in my behavior, in my goodness and my moral standards, then I will judge others who don't measure up. But only Jesus lived a truly holy life, and He did not condemn other people; He had no condemnation to offer. He came to save, not to condemn (John 3:17).

I listen to people's stories when I'm at Soul Care Conferences. People frequently make poor choices, often at least in part because they come from horrible environments. I'm not blaming their environment; I believe you are the only one responsible for you. But I also believe it is a lot harder for someone to make good choices when they grow up under terrible conditions with poor modeling. And I believe that when certain things happen to us, we are more likely to struggle with a particular sin or temptation. When I listen to the story of someone who is struggling with sexual immorality, for example, I often connect the dots of their painful past to their current immoral behavior. In John chapter 4, Jesus had a conversation with the woman at the well. He points out that she has been married five times before, and the guy she is living with now is not her husband. But Jesus doesn't condemn her for her choices; instead, He offers her living water. Essentially, Jesus says to the woman, "I see that you are looking for something that this world hasn't been able to give you. You are empty inside and desperately searching for something to fill the hole in your soul. You are dying of an inner thirst and looking everywhere for a drink that will satisfy your parched and weary soul. I have come to give you that living water that will satisfy the inner emptiness you carry."

Jesus doesn't have condemnation or judgment for this woman; He knows her life has led to an inner emptiness that has motivated her to make poor choices in an attempt to quench her spiritual thirst. He doesn't excuse her choices, but He does display compassion for her soul. She has been seeking to fill the emptiness and heal the pain she carries. Is she morally responsible for her choices? Absolutely. Yet Jesus doesn't judge her; rather, He offers her an answer for her heart's deepest longing. He sees the pain motivating her immoral choices and is moved with compassion for her broken and weary soul. He came to help broken people—people like you and me. This is the way I want to be. I am so inspired by Jesus' tender compassion for broken people who make poor choices—that is the way I want to live. I don't want to be a religious person who carries judgment in my heart toward anyone. When I listen to people's stories, I understand why they have made the choices they have made.

Another problem with performance-based religiosity is that we end up with a privatized religion. We have standards we feel we must meet to be acceptable. There are religious boxes we must check off in order to belong in this community, but when we can't check off all the boxes we're afraid we will be rejected, condemned, and judged. So we keep things to ourselves; we hide, lie, and cover up our sin. We confess things to God but don't live in the light with God and others because of our shame. We keep sinning without repentance, keep confessing without victory, and keep the whole mess private between ourselves and God. We get in a sin/confess cycle, but there is no life change. We're afraid to be open and honest; we are too ashamed to walk in the light with others and too proud to reach out for help. So we end up with a privatized religious faith devoid of transformation.

In contrast, Jesus calls us to be children of the light. John called us to walk in the light with God and others (1 John 1). Paul told us: "You were once darkness, but now you are light in the Lord. Live as children of the light (for the fruit of the light consists in all goodness, righteousness and truth) and find out what pleases the Lord" (Ephesians 5:8-10). When I refuse to walk in the light with God and others, it is because of my pride, and God opposes the proud. Our privatized religion is not the authentic Christian life God has for us or that our hearts long for. This privatized faith will hinder your intimacy with God

> This privatized faith will hinder your intimacy with God and others. We must live as children of the light. Privatized religion produces pride that leads to bondage.

and others. We must live as children of the light. Privatized religion produces pride that leads to bondage.

The number one argument Jesus' disciples had among themselves throughout the gospels was over who might be the greatest. Seriously, doesn't that give you hope? These guys were greatly used by God to change the world, and yet they keep arguing about who was the greatest! In the gospels, they are petty, self-centered people—just like you and me. The night Jesus inaugurated the Lord's Supper with the disciples, after He passed the cup, saying, "This cup is the new covenant in my blood, which is poured out for you," the disciples argued over who was the greatest (Luke 22:20-24)! Wow. Talk about missing it! But don't miss this: the only reason we know that they argued over who is the greatest is because they told us! They had become children of the light! They modeled for us what Jesus wanted in His family. This is authentic faith. Privatized religion is performance-based Christianity that leads to shame, pride, judgment, and bondage. I'll say it again: authentic humility begins with honesty, ends with responsibility, and somewhere in the middle is death to self. We need to humble ourselves before the Lord if we want to draw near to God.

This privatized religious approach often leads us to what Paul called worldly sorrow instead of Godly sorrow (2 Corinthians 7). Worldly sorrow is self-focused: "I am sorry I got caught; I am sorry you think poorly of me now; I am sorry you are upset with me; I am sorry that my reputation has taken a hit; I am sorry I have to live with the consequences of this poor choice." Godly sorrow is others-focused: "I am sorry I have grieved you, Lord, and misrepresented you to others. I am sorry I have done this thing that has hurt the people around me." We have to take our faith out of the private arena if we are going to live an authentic, deep, intimate life in Christ. We have to live as children of the light. And when we live in the light we have more self-awareness, more humility, and more compassion for others.

James said, "'God opposes the proud but shows favor to the humble and oppressed.' Submit yourselves, then, to God. Resist the devil, and he will flee from you. Come near to God and he will come near to you" (James 4:6-8). We cannot draw near to God when we are proud. God is irresistibly attracted to the contrite of heart; the proud walk alone. The devil is trying to tempt us to move in pride, shame, and privatized religion so he can keep us from drawing near to God and living a victorious life. He loves when people are proud; he has them right where he wants them.

Humble yourself before the Lord. Look first to your own faults, then to the faults of others. Be honest about your own faults with others. The more you see your faults, and talk about your faults with others, the more you'll find God's grace for you and draw near to God's presence. Now, please, don't take pride in your faults! Own them humbly and seek to represent Jesus better with the help of the Spirit.

> The more you see your faults, and talk about your faults with others, the more you'll find God's grace for you and draw near to God's presence.

One of the ways I know I'm falling into the religious performance trap is when I'm slow to apologize to others or when I find myself groveling before God because of my sin. If I am slow to apologize to others, that is obviously pride. Be slow to sin but quick to admit wrong-doing. Be slow to defend but quick to listen and own whatever you can own. These are things I think about and try to live out, and when I fail to live them out, I go back and apologize as soon as I realize my wrongdoing. There have also been times I have come to the Lord more than once for the same sin; I committed it once, but I've confessed it multiple times. These

> I cannot earn forgiveness. I cannot beg hard enough, do enough penance, or confess it frequently enough that I deserve to be forgiven.

are signs I'm trying to earn my way back to God; I am motivated by shame, not authentic humility. I cannot earn forgiveness. I cannot beg hard enough, do enough penance, or confess it frequently enough that I deserve to be forgiven. I need to simply stop making it too much about me and look to Jesus. My only hope for forgiveness and reconciliation to God is Jesus' death and resurrection. We know that cognitively, but are we living it authentically? We know the verses—like Romans 8:1 and 1 John 1:9. We can quote them. But when we keep coming back to God for the same thing we already confessed, while we know these verses, we aren't experiencing their reality. Sometimes this is because we are not walking in the light with God and others. Humbling ourselves and being honest can help set us free. Other times it is because we are carrying shame, and shame is just pride wrapped in self-disgust. We are still making it too much about us. We are acting as if we should have been better than that, but we aren't better than that—that's why we need a Savior! We must move into

authentic humility and receive what God has graciously of-
fered.

Head Knowledge Versus Heart Experience
**Last, religion focuses on head knowledge over heart expe-
rience.** Religious people all too often focus on doctrine to the
unfortunate exclusion of matters of the heart. They emphasize
truth over love—even though Jesus said love is the most important thing. Truth matters, but not at the expense of love.
Too often religious people shame and berate others in arguments over theological minutiae and miss the primary objec-
tive to love well. They argue over things that are secondary
doctrines, as though they are primary doctrines, and cannot
discern the difference. You can never have a conversation with
these types of people that is productive because they always
must have the last word.

In the beginning I tried to reason with religious people
who would attack me on matters like deliverance. I tried to
find common footing in our primary beliefs and allow secondary issues to take a secondary position. But they couldn't
agree to disagree. Even though we both loved Jesus, believed
the Bible was true, held to the truth that Jesus is the only way,
and were in accord on every major doctrine—none of it mattered. Many of these people went on to attack me and call me
a heretic, a false teacher, and assorted other names. I tried to
reason with them about why I believe what I believe, only to
be attacked further. I tried to say, "Let's focus on the things
we agree about and agree to disagree on this matter," only to
be told I was wrong and that they could not agree to disagree
because I was compromising the truth. What truth? Their

version of the truth? So I simply stopped engaging. I realized there was no winning. They always had to have the last word; they always had to win. They were always right, never wrong, and they could not graciously agree to disagree. When people would write me long emails attacking me, or write against me in public forums, or rail against me on FaceBook, or blog against me, or give a nasty review at some book forum saying I am a false teacher or heretic, I would simply say to Jen, "I am too busy casting out demons to chase phantoms." I cannot be bothered with these arguments anymore.

In Luke 11 Jesus casts out a demon from a man who was mute, and the mute man talks. Yet some people said Jesus cast out the demons by the power of Beelzebul, and "others tested him by asking for a sign from Heaven" (Luke 11:16). Please don't miss this: a mute guy gets a demon cast out and can now talk, and they want a *sign from Heaven?* The evidence of the power of deliverance ministry is found in life change. Yet I've talked to people who admit they have seen life change in the people who have come to a Soul Care Conference and seen others go through a deliverance, but they are unwilling to admit it was because of the deliverance that the life changed. The people who were delivered testified that this was the reason for their life change, but those who were attacking wouldn't listen—it was outside their theological box, and everyone who disagreed with their thinking was wrong despite any evidence to the contrary. That's why I stopped engaging in the argument, because they were not sincerely seeking or asking. They were so looking to win a fight from their preconceived set of beliefs that they were not willing to re-examine their presuppositions in the face of plain evidence.

We can believe all the right things about God, have orthodox doctrine, say all the right things, and even do the right things, yet still have hearts that are far from God. "These people honor me with their lips, but their hearts are far from me" (Matthew 15:8). I want to have good doctrine. I want to believe the truth. I have studied the Scriptures my whole life, and I am passionate about being faithful to the Word of God. I have read the Bible cover to cover hundreds of times. I have a Master's in Divinity and a Doctorate in Ministry focused on exegetical preaching that is rooted in the Word of God; I have centered my life on Jesus and taken truth seriously. But if I am obsessed with being right, and not with loving well, something is seriously wrong with my faith. If I am not humble enough to admit there are other views out there on many interpretations of Scripture, if I can't agree to disagree with honor and dignity, then I am proud and religious. If I'm convinced I am always right in my theological view, and feel the need to oppose those who disagree with me, that's the spirit of religion. If I find my purpose in heresy hunting, not in loving like Jesus, then my faith is closer to the Pharisees than it is to Jesus. I have many views on doctrinal issues that I hold deeply, but I do not read the books of people who disagree with me and go out and post against them. Why would I do that? Why would I believe it is my job to offer correction to everyone I disagree with? I'm too busy trying to advance Jesus' kingdom to bother with attacking others who Jesus died for.

> If I find my purpose in heresy hunting, not in loving like Jesus, then my faith is closer to the Pharisees than it is to Jesus.

God looks at the heart. 1 Samuel 16:7: "The Lord does not look at the things that human beings look at. People look at the outward appearance, but the Lord looks at the heart." When He looks at my heart, at your heart, what does He see? Does He see humility in us? Does He see love in us? Does He see contrition? Are we quick to apologize and admit wrong? Do we always have to have the last word and win every battle? Can we agree to disagree and treat people we disagree with honorably? What does God see when He looks at our heart? I want God to find humility and love in my heart above all things.

I think one of the reasons we've become so "heady" in our faith is because the Western world is a very knowledge-based learning atmosphere. We sit in classrooms where a teacher lectures us, and we have to give back the right answers on a test. The right knowledge allows us to advance—we get to the next level, the next achievement, the next degree, the next certificate, the next job, the next promotion and raise. But the kingdom works differently than the world. Jesus wasn't a knowledge-based discipleship teacher; He was an obedience-based discipleship Lord. He wasn't asking us simply to listen to what He said and be able to regurgitate the right answers on a final exam. He was asking us to integrate what He said into our daily lives. This is why, so often, we ask the wrong questions. We ask people, "Do you know your identity in Christ?" or "Do you know you are loved by God?" Instead, we should be asking, "Are you living like a deeply loved person in all of your relational interactions?" The first question is about knowledge; the second is about integration. We ask others, "Are you spending time with God?" Or "Are you doing your devotions?" Instead, we should be asking, "Is your spiritual rhythm working? Are the spiritual practices you're engaging in drawing you close to God? Are you becoming more loving? Do you love God more and love people more? Are you more free and full in life?" The first set of questions, once again, is about knowledge; the second set is about integration. Religion simplifies complex things and leads us to overly simplistic black-and-white thinking.

If we are going to move from religion to an authentic Christian experience, we're going to have to move from the head to the heart, from knowledge to integration (or obedience), from understanding to experiential living. If we are going to get there, we must ask better questions. We must ask questions that drive integration and obedience, not ones that merely measure knowledge and behavior. We must ask questions that demonstrate the realities of the heart, not merely the externals.

Just to be clear: I am not suggesting we move away from core doctrines of the faith—not at all. I believe we need to guard the truth. Paul told Timothy, "Preach the word; be prepared in season and out of season; correct, rebuke and encourage—with great patience and careful instruction. For the time will come when people will not put up with sound doctrine" (2 Timothy 4:3). I believe there are a set of core beliefs passed down through the ages that are orthodox and essential and, if we are to be faithful, we must hold to those. However, if we hold to those without love, do we represent Jesus well? Not at all. If we hold to those and a bunch of others that are not essential and berate those who disagree with us on these non-essential doctrines, does that represent Jesus well? No. If we hold onto all the essential doctrines but don't integrate Jesus' teachings into our daily lives, and do not love like Jesus loves, nor live like Jesus lives, are we mature? No. The measure of maturity isn't merely good doctrine. We must get beyond this.

Take time to pause and ask God to show you if there are any religious ways in you. The following are all great questions to spend some time with.

Where do you see fear creeping into your spiritual journey? Is there any pride in your relationship with God and others? Are you quick to admit wrong with God? Are you walking in the light with God and others? Are you readily admitting and apologizing for your wrongdoing with others? Are you slow to defend yourself and quick to apologize? Has control made its way into your spiritual life and practices? Have you taken on holiness standards that are beyond the standards of God? Are you wrestling with judgment of others who don't meet your standards? Are you free from shame? Are you humbly bringing your sin to God and walking in the light with others? Is there any pattern of privatized religion that leaves you in shame, pride, and judgment? Are you measuring your spiritual maturity by matters of the heart or by issues of performance, behavior, and external standards? Do you feel the need to argue with others about doctrines and persuade them to your way of thinking? Are you looking for where people are wrong doctrinally, or where they are right with God? Are you asking the right questions of your faith? Is your heart expanding in love for God and others? Are you living free and full in Christ? Are you experiencing love, joy, and peace through the Spirit? Is there any fear in you about the things of the Spirit?

Two

DRAWING NEAR

So how do we draw near to God? How do we make the shift from learned behaviors to authentic experience, from privatized religion to deep transformation, from knowledge to revelation, from passive belief to active trust?

How do we develop authentic, deep intimacy with God?

Everyone who attempts to walk with God has some religious tendencies and can fall into the trap of religion. You have to start by realizing this truth. There have been times I have read two chapters of Scripture and had no idea what I was reading because my mind was on something else. I was going through the religious exercise of reading my Bible—a good discipline—but was distracted and falling into a routine without real meaning. That's religion. I have gone to church after an argument with my wife and been greeted by someone at the door with, "How are you?" And I then replied, "I'm fine, thank you. How are you?" That's the way religion operates.

I have spent time in silence trying to fix my loving attention on Jesus—and have caught myself ten minutes into this solitude not having thoughts of Jesus at all because I was thinking about something else. Something far less important. That's religion.

When we practice religious practices without our hearts set on meeting Jesus afresh, loving Jesus more deeply, and following Jesus more completely, we often become more religious and less like Jesus. The purpose of reading our Bible isn't to know the Bible; the purpose of reading the Bible is to encounter the living God. This is true of all the spiritual disciplines: they are a means to an end, not an end in themselves. The Pharisees practiced all these disciplines, but in the end, they killed Jesus. That's religion at its very worst. We want to make sure our practices leave us knowing and being more like Jesus.

In many of my other books I have written about how to develop intimacy with Jesus through spiritual practices. I've talked about this in different ways in *Pathways to the King*, *River Dwellers*, *Deep Faith*, *Spiritual Authority*, and *The Soul Care Leader*. You can refer to those books for help in developing a healthy spiritual rhythm that takes you deeper in intimacy with God.

With this book, however, I want to do something different. I want to talk about the nature of intimacy, how it works, and apply it to our relationship with God.

Intimacy

Let's think of intimacy in terms of four necessary components: **self-discovery**, **self-disclosure**, **vulnerability**, and **self-**

control. Let me explain these four components of intimacy, and then we will apply them to our relationship with God.

For two people to develop intimacy there must be **self-discovery**; there has to be growth and development. If Jen and I are not growing in maturity, learning new things about ourselves, and growing in self-awareness, our intimacy will be stunted. We will be telling the same old story to one another, and if there is nothing new to say, nothing new to share, nothing new to learn about each other, we will grow stale in our relationship. So for intimacy to go deeper there must be a sense of both parties growing in self-awareness.

Second, we have to risk **sharing what we are discovering** about ourselves if we are going to draw near one another. If I'm learning new things about myself, but I am not willing to disclose what I have discovered with Jen, I may be growing in self-awareness, but Jen and I are not growing in intimacy. If I am willing to disclose with Jen, but I am not growing, not learning anything new, then our attempts at developing intimacy are going to be thwarted by my lack of growth. There must be both self-discovery and self-disclosure—by both parties—for intimacy to flourish.

The third component of intimacy is **vulnerability**. We cannot draw near to one another without it. There is a difference between transparency and vulnerability. I am very honest in both my writing and speaking. Nearly every conference I speak in, I have people approach me and say, "I feel like I know you because I've read your books." But they don't really know me; they know about me. It's the same when I am speaking: I am honest, open, and confessional. People feel like they are connected to me, and tell me so, because of that. But again, they don't really know me, they know about me. I'm being transparent with people, but I am not really being vulnerable with that individual. There is a difference. I can be transparent with you—open and honest—without really entrusting myself to you in relational intimacy. If I am open and honest, but I don't expect anything back from you, that is transparency without vulnerability. I don't expect you to be there for me, care for me, meet my needs, or treat me with dignity and respect. In the same way, in a personal relationship with you, I can be transparent without being vulnerable, and it will hinder us from connecting deeply. But when I am honest and vulnerable . . . now I am laying my heart out there, and I have an expectation that you will be there for me, you will care for me, you will be empathetic, loving, and respectful. If you are not willing to meet my expectation, I am going to be deeply hurt. That is true vulnerability. If I am transparent, but not vulnerable—not exposing my heart with expectation of you—then I am not going to be as hurt when you don't meet me with compassion. There are people who are transparent yet remain invulnerable, and when people try to get close to them, they feel an intimacy barrier.

If I am open with Jen, but I am still not expecting anything from her because I am living with some guardedness and self-protection, then Jen will have this strange feeling that I am being confessional, but that I am not truly letting her in. She will have a sense that I am a little "plastic" with her—untouchable, invulnerable. This will prevent us from drawing near to one another. I have often had this feeling with religious people. It is common for religious people to be closed and not confessional; however, when Soul Care is introduced into a religious atmosphere, people often realize they are now expected to be honest and confessional to be accepted in this context. They become honest so they can play by the set of religious rules and expectations being introduced in their community. But even when they are honest with me, I can sense they are not completely honest; they are still not being vulnerable. They are hiding behind a wall of self-protection and not truly confiding in anyone else either. Sadly, often they do not know they are self-protected, but those around them sense it. They haven't truly broken free from privatized religion; they just brought a little bit of stuff out of the darkness into the light because that is what they need to do to belong in this new religious culture. This is why I say to pastors that you cannot just lay Soul Care over a religious culture; you have to intentionally dismantle the religious culture before you start to implement a Soul Care culture. (I cover this in my book *The Soul Care Leader*.)

The final component of intimacy is **self-control**; this component is about changing. Listen: if I discover I am doing something in my relationship with Jen that is hurting her, and I discover why I do what I do, and I talk openly about this with Jen, but I do not change, then we are going to have a hard time moving forward in intimacy. I am violating trust by my hurtful behavior, and we cannot develop intimacy without trust. If I discover I am a jerk, and disclose that I am a jerk, but continue to do jerky things without any life change, then our relational closeness is in jeopardy. Self-control,

> Self-control, which Paul lists in the fruit of the Spirit, is necessary in the process of sanctification; it is the life change process through which we take responsibility for our lives.

which Paul lists in the fruit of the Spirit, is necessary in the process of sanctification; it is the life change process through which we take responsibility for our lives and, with the help of the Holy Spirit, create new life patterns. In relationships, this is essential for developing intimacy. Life change allows us to have increasingly healthier interactions, and this deepens trust, love, and intimacy.

So these are the four key components of relational intimacy: **self-discovery, self-disclosure, vulnerability,** and **self-control**. This is how intimacy works. Now I want to think about this as it pertains to our relationship with God.

Intimacy with God

In one of my favorite passages, the Apostle John writes, "God is light; in him there is no darkness at all. If we claim to have fellowship with him and yet walk in the darkness, we lie and do not live out the truth. But if we walk in the light, as he is in the light, we have fellowship with one another, and the blood of Jesus, his Son, purifies us from all sin" (1 John 1:5-7). I want to make note of several things in this passage as it relates to **self-discovery and intimacy**.

First, God doesn't have any self-discovery to make: He is light, and in Him there is no darkness. There is nothing God doesn't already know about Himself. So God doesn't have to discover new things about Himself, but we discover new things about God, and God reveals new things about Himself to us so we can draw nearer to Him.

Second, we need to discover new things about ourselves if we are going to continue to draw near to God. God, obviously, already knows these things about us, and He wants to reveal them to us. If we refuse to receive the light God offers and to admit that we have darkness within us, we cannot walk close to God, who is light. God shines light into our souls to help us with this self-discovery process; He not only reveals Himself to us, He also reveals *ourselves* to us. God never shines light into the suitcase of our soul to make us feel bad; God shines light to get us free and help us draw near to Him. But if we refuse the light God offers us as a gift, we are rejecting God Himself, who is light. We cannot reject the light God offers and draw near to God. Self-discovery is essential for developing intimacy with God because we are becoming children of the light.

Third, John rejects the notion of privatized religion. If we are really in the light with God, then we will be in the light with other believers. If we are not willing to be in the light with others, it is because we are proud—we want to look better than we are, and God opposes the proud. We cannot be proud, or self-protected, and draw near to God.

Self-Discovery

The problem with many of us who have spent a lot of time in religious settings is that we lack self-awareness and don't know it. When Jen and I got married, I thought I was reasonably healthy. I grew up in a decent home, better than most of my friends, and was doing many of the right things. I read my Bible, prayed, went to church, and was trying to treat my wife kindly. I wasn't acting abusively or immorally. I was even doing a lot of the right relational things; we were talking and processing conflicts together. But we got stuck, and we got stuck precisely because we knew less than we thought

> We were stuck because we were not as healthy as I thought we were. If you think you don't need it, you won't go there.

we knew about ourselves. People often say, "What you don't know won't hurt you." But the reality of the soul is that what you don't know about yourself is killing you, and it is killing those around you. The only one I was responsible for was me. I had to go deeper into self-awareness if Jen and I were going to have breakthroughs in our relationship. The realization that it takes two healthy people to have a healthy relationship, and that we were stuck because we were not as healthy as I thought we were, was critical to growing in self-awareness. If you think you don't need it, you won't go there.

I have people come to me all the time who are wrestling with issues—relational conflicts, anxiety, depression, addiction, sin patterns, or some other presenting problem—and they say to me, "I am very self-aware." They are self-aware about their presenting issues, but as I ask questions, I realize they have no self-awareness about why they do what they do or why they are experiencing the things they are. My favorite Soul Care question is, "What's underneath that?" Why do you do what you do, feel what you feel, act the way you act, think the way you think? Jesus said, "For out of the overflow of the heart the mouth speaks" (Matthew 12:34). Later Jesus said, "The things that come out of the mouth come from the heart, and these defile you. For out of the heart come evil thoughts, murder, adultery, sexual immorality, theft, false testimony, slander" (Matthew 15:18, 19). We must get to the matters of the heart if we are going to walk in the light with God and draw near to Him. The Pharisees cleaned up the outside of the dish but ignored the issues of the heart. We have to get deeper.

As I travel the world, one thing that I can tell you characterizes religious places and religious people is a very low level of self-awareness. Many people have not plumbed the depths of the heart and soul. Jesus said of the Pharisees that they were focused on the outside, not the inside. Sadly, a lot of this is because religion produces a culture of shallow living. We measure things by external standards, and we miss the heart and soul—that's what happened with the Pharisees. Externals are easier to evaluate, manage, and control. The matters of the heart are much more difficult to assess, see, understand, and change. So, in church, we are taught the right doctrines, right phrases, and right behaviors to fit in. Too often, we measure maturity by our knowledge. If you know the right answers, you are mature. So people play by the rules, give the right answers, and live in shallow waters of limited authentic Christian experience. We must get to the heart and soul if we are going to get into the deep waters with God. He is light, and He is not merely concerned with your behaviors; He is concerned with your heart. He is not trying to show you what is in your heart to make you feel bad; He wants to heal your soul and set you free.

> Many people have not plumbed the depths of the heart and soul. Jesus said of the Pharisees that they were focused on the outside, not the inside.

So how can we get to the deeper matters of the heart? How do we become people of self-awareness and self-discovery? Let me cover two practical areas to help us. First, we will cover some hindrances to self-discovery that we need to address. Second, we'll talk about some practices that can take us into deeper self-discovery.

Hindrances to Self-Discovery

The first hindrance on our journey to self-discovery is pride. Often, we are unwilling to see the truth about ourselves. Sometimes that is because of shame; other times it is because of our insecurity. But insecurity, shame, and pride all make it too much about us; they are all rooted in self-focus. When we are proud, we do not have eyes to see and ears to hear, as Jesus says. We must be willing to humble ourselves before the Lord. Authentic humility begins with honesty. It takes humility to see your sin, brokenness, dysfunction, and flaws; it takes humility to admit these things and take responsibility for them, and it takes humility to die to self and surrender to God.

In my relationship with Jen, in the beginning, when she confronted me about something, I defended myself because of pride, insecurity, and shame. I was slow to admit the truth about myself. It was hindering me on my journey to self-discovery. Only insecure people are defensive. Secure people don't need to defend themselves; they can admit the truth about themselves because they know they are

> Only insecure people are defensive.

deeply loved by God, and their sense of worth is not threatened. Pride and insecurity will prevent you from admitting your flaws and walking in the light with God. You will deflect the light God offers you as a gift to take you into self-discovery and deeper intimacy because you will see it as a threat. You will resort to image management and self-protection instead of self-discovery. When I discovered this truth, I decided not to defend myself in my conversations with Jen. That was a key turning point—it opened me up to learn new things about myself. I had a breakthrough in self-discovery when I let go of my pride and self-protection.

Now, I have made it my practice to fight against my insecurity and pride, but make no mistake—doing so isn't easy. When I was a pastor, if someone confronted me on an issue, I sought to listen without defending myself. If I could clearly see that I did something wrong, I owned it and apologized. If, however, I didn't feel like I had done anything wrong, rather than defending myself, I said to the person, "I am going to pray about this, and I will get back to you." Then I asked God if anything that person said was true; I humbled myself before the Lord and listened to Him because I knew I could be guilty of easily deflecting the truth about myself. If, after praying, I still didn't feel like it was true about me, I would take it before a couple of friends and say, without revealing the person's name, "Someone said this about me, and I would like your honest perspective. Is this true about me?" These were people who loved me and would tell me the truth. If one of them said it was true, I would ask them to help me see it, and then I went back to the person and owned what I needed to. If none of them felt it was true, I would go back to the original person and say, "I have prayed about it. I asked a few people who love me and tell me the truth, but I am still not sensing this is true about me." They then knew I took them seriously, and I felt like I had really processed the matter and made sure I wasn't too quick to dismiss something I needed to hear.

I found this process of fighting my base instinct to defend, deflect, and deny the truth an incredible aid to self-discovery. You have to lay down your pride if you are going to discover the truth about yourself.

The second hindrance to self-discovery is self-protection. This desire to protect ourselves may come from our insecurity and shame, and often it comes out of some unprocessed wounding. We were hurt along the way, and we built up walls of self-protection so we wouldn't continue getting hurt. The problem is that when we have walls up for so long they become normal for us. Sadly, I am not a naturally neat person. I can easily allow some clutter to go unnoticed because it has been there a while, and it is now part of the landscape. It doesn't seem out of place any longer; it seems normal. So it is with our self-protection; we have held onto it for a long time and it becomes normal to us. We no longer notice it. But sadly, it is hindering us from going deeper with God because it is keeping us from self-discovery.

It is not uncommon for me to say to someone at a Soul Care Conference, "You know you are self-protected, right?" Sometimes the person laughs nervously, sometimes they bristle a little. In these situations, the person has come to me for help because of some presenting issue; I am not saying this to hurt the person. This is what the person must address if they are going to experience breakthrough. They have to let down their walls of self-protection so they can come into self-awareness. On more than one occasion the person has responded by saying, "No. I don't think so." I respond, "Has your spouse ever said to you that you are self-protective?" They admitted the spouse had, but the person was unwilling to address it.

If you have been wounded growing up, and we all have, then you likely have some measures of self-protection. They served you well when you were young, but now it is time to address them to move forward. At this point, they are only "protecting" you now from self-awareness and the road to intimacy. So how do you protect yourself? Are you defensive? passive-aggressive? angry? silent? controlling? manipulative? Do you withdraw? Do you avoid conflict, uncomfortable situations, difficult conversations? Do you slip into fantasy instead of diving into painful conversations that can lead to true intimacy? Do you seek to numb the pain with something rather than address the problem? We must discover these self-protective shields and choose not to use them anymore if we are going to come to new levels of self-awareness and intimacy.

I was having a conversation with someone recently who told me they suspected they had been sexually abused. I asked this person if they were willing to face the possibility and discover the truth. This person said—as I have heard hundreds of times before—"Do I have to? I don't want to know. Can't I get better without knowing?" They didn't want to go there because it was terrifying, and they wanted to use denial to protect themselves from the pain. But you cannot heal that which you will not admit. God is light; in Him there is no darkness. So if we are going to grow up in Christ and grow deep in Christ, we must be willing to let go of our self-protective measures that keep us from walking in the light. In the end, the person went to that difficult place, and it has radically changed their life. The next

> You cannot heal that which you will not admit. God is light; in Him there is no darkness.

time I saw them, the person was aglow with God and told me they have never felt so free, full, and fulfilled in life and marriage. That's why we must let go of our self-protection.

A third area that keeps us from self-discovery is that some of us grew up in an environment that didn't encourage self-awareness, and we don't know how to get there. We haven't developed processing skills. I often see this, for example, in rural areas because, for many generations, the people in these locales have been farmers just trying to survive. Life on the farm is tough, survival can be difficult, and they often don't have time to process their feelings. They have to "suck it up and get over it," and that's what they learn to do, as their ancestors did before them. When this is the pattern generation after generation, no one is taught the skills to process. Many people grow up in families where certain emotions become, essentially, illegal. You aren't allowed to feel sad or angry or depressed or anxious—or whatever emotion is forbidden. When you were a kid and you felt that particular emotion, it wasn't carefully nurtured so that you knew it was a legitimate feeling so you could learn to process it. Rather, it was unwelcomed and dismissed in some way, and you realized you weren't allowed to feel that way, so you learned to shut down the negative emotions. But the more you shut them down, the more shut down you become; you close off certain parts of your heart to yourself, God, and others. You can't move forward without opening up those parts of your heart again.

Multiple times recently I have found myself in environments like this on my travels, and I said to the audience, on more than one occasion, "Do you know that you are a difficult crowd to speak to?" They laughed, and I said, "No, really. Do you know it?" They didn't. I explained that they were not difficult people; they weren't hard-hearted or rebellious or obstinate. But they had grown up in long-standing environments where self-awareness was not valued because of this survival mentality. They hadn't learned how to process, and there is often a spiritual dullness that comes upon a crowd like this. It isn't willful, but they have been avoiding the light that God wants to give, and they must be willing to go there if they want to get to new depths. God is light; any avoidance of the light is a barrier to intimacy with God.

Fourth, sometimes the thing that hinders us from self-discovery is our religion. If we have a privatized religious life and we've been hiding our true selves from others, we are building pride in our hearts. Again, John the Apostle told us, in his letter, that if we are really in the light with God, we will have fellowship with others. The only reason I am not willing to open up to others is because of pride, and God opposes the proud. This privatized faith also keeps us from receiving feedback from others and discovering our blind spots. When people do give us feedback or criticism, we often defend ourselves, counterattack, get passive-aggressive, or withdraw in hurt, but we don't receive it and welcome the light God offers. We have to walk in the light with God and others if we want to journey to self-awareness.

Sometimes we substitute quick, easy religious phrases and cliches for deep authentic processing. The problem is that because we know the phrase, we think we have the experience. When it comes to painful experiences, for example, some people say, "I don't have to deal with that stuff in my past. It is all under the blood." I've heard that hundreds of times. Yes, it's under the blood. But it is also still in the suitcase of your soul! You haven't processed it and gained freedom from it; you are

AUTHENTIC

just tacking a religious phrase over the cancer of your soul like a Band-Aid. I've heard people say, "I don't have to deal with that. I'm a new creature in Christ; the old is gone. The new has come." That's true. But this is describing your potential; it is speaking of your identity in Christ, not saying you don't have to deal with your issues. The Corinthian church Paul was writing to was fraught with a host of issues that needed to be addressed. Paul wasn't asking his listeners to tack on religious phrases as excuses not to deal with their issues. That would not be authentic.

The New Testament uses different verb tenses for our salvation experience. We *have been saved* (past tense, it is finished); we are being saved (present tense, we are working out our salvation with fear and trembling); we will be saved (future tense, we will become like Him when we get to Heaven). Indeed, we are new creatures in Christ. That has been accomplished by Jesus on the cross, and it is our potential to live in freedom because of what Jesus has done, but we are working that out in our day-to-day lives (we are being saved). Paul never intended these realities to be used as religious phrases that would keep people from dealing with their issues and maturing. That's just religion. The verses that talk about what Christ has done for us are about his finished work and our potential for living, but they are only realized in

> Paul never intended these realities to be used as religious phrases that would keep people from dealing with their issues and maturing. That's just religion.

the present tense of working out our salvation with fear and trembling. Again, the question is: are you living this out?

In the holiness tradition I am part of, many people have used the phrase "the deeper life" to describe walking in the presence, power, and purity of the Holy Spirit. But it became a phrase with little experiential meaning attached to it for many people in the movement. It became words without reality, doctrine without depth—and that is religion. Many people kept the phrase but didn't update their experiences. Or, in some tribes, people talk about the filling or baptism of the Spirit. In Pentecostal circles, that experience is often associated with tongues, and people will often look back to an experience they had twenty years ago when they encountered God and spoke in tongues, and they often have the mentality that they are all set because they spoke in tongues. But, again, we have to ask the right questions. In these tribes we often ask, "Were you filled with the Holy Spirit?" Or, possibly, "Do you speak in tongues?" Those are okay to ask. But here is a better question: "Are you currently walking in the fullness of the Spirit?" And, "Are you experiencing the ongoing presence, power, and purification of the Spirit?" Not: "Are you speaking in tongues?" Not, "Were you filled with the Spirit?" But, "How is it impacting your life right now?" Yes, I want you to have encounters with the Spirit. But are you currently walking in that fullness?

I was teaching a doctoral class one day and ended up doing deliverance on a brother who was from a Pentecostal background. Later in the day I prayed for him, and he fell out on the floor and was filled with the Holy Spirit in a fresh, demonstrative, and powerful way. Afterward he came to me and my friend Martin and said, "You guys are more Pentecostal than my Pentecostal denomination." I knew his tribe, and have done conferences with them before, and I knew his observation was true because too often they had learned behaviors and right phrases substituting for authentic current experiences.

When we are going through hardships, too often we throw out religious phrases and cliches instead of processing the pain deeply and getting to the authentic. In my book *Calm in the Storm*, I wrote, "If we don't process our grief, our trust will be diminished. We can't whitewash pain and heartache with pithy religious phrases or a memorized verse from the Bible. This is what a religious person does—they take a truth and put it on like an outer garment, but they fail to internalize it in their inner being so that it becomes part of their life. They have the right words, but religion is skin-deep. Religious people often fail to internalize eternal truths, and they face life with a thin soul. True trust is developed when hardships are authentically processed and the pain-stricken heart comes to restful surrender in the eternal arms of the Man of Sorrows" (*Calm in the Storm*, Amazon, 2020, pp. 64, 65).

Sometimes religious people over-spiritualize issues, and this limits their self-discovery. In my previous role as a professor, there were times I received papers that were so full of religious jargon that there was no true substance or any display of self-awareness. There was no real, authentic, honest communication taking place. If I took out all the religious jargon, you wouldn't actually discover anything about the person who wrote the paper except that there is little authentic depth there; there is merely a mask of religion. Trying to get someone to see this and break free from this has proven incredibly difficult. People have become so entrenched in the language of religion that they have confused it with authentic experience. Sometimes the over-spiritualizing is expressed as if every-

> People have become so entrenched in the language of religion that they have confused it with authentic experience.

thing is an attack from the enemy. To be clear, I believe in the spiritual realm, and I believe in Satan and demons, but some things are just human. Not everything is a spiritual attack. Sometimes we find ourselves in difficult situations in a Christian organization because we have made poor leadership decisions. We aren't getting attacked by Satan because we are a church or a Christian organization; we have just blown it as leaders. Sometimes we are struggling in our marriage not because Satan is attacking us because we are in a Christian marriage, but because we are emotionally unhealthy people who make decisions that create chaos in our lives. That's not Satan; that's just human. This over-spiritualization keeps us from taking responsibility for our lives and moving ahead with authentic life change.

Over-spiritualizing issues also leads to over-simplification. Simplistic thinking, once again, limits our capacity to see the truth and take responsibility, so it becomes hard to develop depth. When people oversimplify, they see things as black and white, but not everything is black and white; some things are gray. Not everything is simple. Some things are complex, and they require a much deeper, more complex form of thinking. Let me use anxiety as an example. Some people view anxiety in a simplistic way and say, "They just need to trust God." Sounds spiritual, but life isn't always that simple. Others view anxiety and say, "It is anxiety disorder, and they need counseling and maybe medications." That, also, can be too simplistic. Both of these could be true—or neither could be true. The person may be wrestling with anxiety because they are not firmly established in their identity. They could be struggling with anxiety because they don't have good boundaries and have taken on too much in life. They may have demonic issues at the root of their anxiety and need deliverance to be set free. These are just a handful of the issues that could be at stake, and it could be a complex blend of multiple things. When we oversimplify, we fail to address the root issues, we lack wisdom, and we miss out on maturity and intimacy.

Practices of Self-Discovery

How do we break free and move forward in self-discovery? Let me lay out some helpful practices to consider.

First, if we want to grow in self-discovery, it helps to take regular time to reflect and process. In the early days of our first marriage struggle, I learned how to spend time alone with God and reflect, with the help of the Holy Spirit, on my behaviors, feelings, thoughts, and motives. I often had to wrestle with God about why I did what I did, felt what I felt, and thought the way I thought. I invited God to reveal things to me, show me the truth about myself, and search me and know me, as David said in Psalm 139. I wrestled a lot with the question, "What's underneath that?" I was trying to get to the heart and soul motivations, not merely focus on the externals. This wrestling took time. The Lord knows who we are, how we got to be the way we are, and what is driving our thinking, feelings, and behavior. He wants to show us. God never shines light into our hearts to make us feel bad; God shines light to set us free. Light is a welcome guest, not an intruder. I had to fight

This wrestling took time. The Lord knows who we are, how we got to be the way we are, and what is driving our thinking, feelings, and behavior. He wants to show us.

against my base instinct to rationalize, justify, defend, deny, and spin, all in trying to protect myself. I had to learn that these were tools to keep me from freedom. Linger in God's presence and let Him show you things about yourself; resist the urge to fight against the light. For some of us, this is hard to do because we have built up many walls of self-protection, including religion and Christian jargon. Sometimes we need other people outside our circle to help us break free, and we must determine to receive feedback without defensiveness.

Second, if we are going to grow in self-awareness, we need to process our negative emotions regularly with God and others. Nearly 40 percent of the Psalms are lament Psalms in which David or the other psalmists process their negative emotions. They are a great model for us to follow. I have often used the lament Psalms to help me get in touch with my emotions. I read through several Psalms until I find one that resonates with my emotional state of being, and I pray it back to God with my own words and through the lens of my own experience and circumstances. This practice has often helped me give voice to the things I feel. I pray through my negative emotions every day. I have discovered my negative emotions are often an early indicator that something is off in my soul. Processing them is vital to health, self-awareness, and freedom. In my book *The Soul Care Leader*, I have written more about how to process in a way that leads to breakthrough.

Third, to grow in self-discovery we need to keep our spiritual rhythm fresh. When our routine becomes a rut, we become religious. When I am encountering God, experiencing God's presence, hearing God's voice, and walking in the light with God and others, I am much more likely to be growing in self-awareness. I have written often about how to keep your rhythm fresh; see *The Soul Care Leader* and *River Dwellers* for more help.

> I pray through my negative emotions every day. I have discovered my negative emotions are often an early indicator that something is off in my soul.

Ask yourself the right question. Not "Are you spending time with God?" But "Is your rhythm working?" How do you know if your rhythm is working? Here are some things to consider: are you loving God and people more this year than last year? Are you sensing God's presence, hearing God's voice, and walking in freedom and fullness? Often when our rhythm becomes stagnant, we become stuck spiritually, and we are prone to fall into the rut of religion. I have discovered that change and sacrifice are vital to getting "unstuck" in our spiritual rhythm.

Fourth, we have to intentionally cultivate humility. Take every opportunity to humble yourself. Own all you can—with God and others. Always seek to see your part and own it, even if the other person doesn't own his or her part. Put defensiveness to death. When you feel defensive, own what you should and go back and listen to the person with a determination that, because you are secure in God's love, you will not defend yourself. When we walk in authentic humility, our hearts are positioned to grow.

Fifth, if you want to grow in self-discovery, expose yourself to the right books and the right people. Read books that address the issues of the heart and soul. Read books that move things past the head into the realm of experience with God and help you access God's presence. Read books that move past having the right answers to having the right heart before God. Read books that help you love God and love people more. Read books that move your heart to be tender before God. Don't just read books for more knowledge—do the hard work of processing. And spend time with people who focus on knowing God, not knowing about God. Spend time with people who are focused more on loving God and loving people well than they are on talking about their opinions on all sorts of matters. Spend time with people who are honest, open, and confessional, and join them living in the light. If you don't know people like this already, invite some people to join you on the journey to become like this together!

Self-Disclosure

If we are going to grow in intimacy with God and others, not only must we grow in self-awareness, we must disclose the things we discover. This is as true in our relationship with God as it is in our relationships with other people. As I said earlier, God doesn't need to discover new things about Himself; He already knows all things. But God does choose to reveal new things about Himself to us because He wants us to know Him better. He also wants to continue to reveal new things to us about ourselves. God doesn't need us to reveal things about ourselves to Him so He can learn about us—He already knows. He wants us to do this so that we humble ourselves before Him. Humility welcomes the presence of God in intimacy. Let's talk about some of the hindrances and helps that can aid us in our journey to self-disclosure.

Hindrances to Self-Disclosure

One of the things that keeps us from receiving God's self-disclosure is our approach to God. Sometimes I get stuck in a rut in my spiritual rhythm, and my time with God is not fresh. I have read the Bible cover to cover dozens of times, and some sections of Scripture I have read hundreds of times. If I am not careful, I can come to my Scripture reading with what I already know and without being open to fresh revelation. If I come to a familiar passage with preconceived notions, and my theological framework, I can read it with an "I know that" attitude and miss out on God's fresh word for me that day.

I meditate on Scripture regularly to keep my time with God fresh. I wait for that "God-breathed" moment when I sense the Holy Spirit stirring a particular phrase or portion of a passage, and I linger there to see what the Spirit is saying to me. This morning I was meditating on Matthew 9:9-13, where Jesus calls Matthew to follow Him. It is a passage I have read hundreds of times. The phrase that struck me this morning was "Learn what this means: 'I desire mercy, not sacrifice'" (Matthew 9:13). I lingered there with Jesus. The Pharisees were upset that Jesus was eating with tax collectors and sinners because they viewed these people as vile and despicable. But what God really desires from us is not all our religious offerings, sacrifices, church activities, and spiritual practices, unless they lead us to love people with more of God's tenderness. I want to have Jesus' heart for people who are far from God—even when they are doing things that are dark and evil. Jesus loves them and wants them to repent and come to Him.

Another thing that keeps me from discovering new things about God is when my prayer time becomes a monological rut in which I keep saying the same things to God over and over. If I'm having a one-way conversation with God, and I keep praying the same prayers each day, that is not going to lead me to new levels of intimacy. I am not learning anything new, nor am I discovering anything new about God. Neither am I giving God an opportunity to disclose more things to me about Himself. I have to open up space for God to speak to me—through the Scriptures and through the Holy Spirit. If you want to know more about hearing God's voice, in my book *River Dwellers* I have an entire chapter on how to do so. I have also found that praying Scriptures over my life and family has been a helpful path to make my prayer time new and fresh. I have spent an entire year, for example, praying the epistles over our family. I read a chapter and prayed through the phrases, concepts, and truths that were most relevant for us.

Sometimes we face hindrances in our self-disclosure to God. Our pride and image management can not only hinder us from intimacy with people, it can also hinder us in intimacy with God. Without authentic humility we will never reveal ourselves fully to God. In the Luke 19 parable of the Pharisee and the tax collector that I referenced earlier in the book, the Pharisee talks about how good he is, and how bad the tax collector is, but his pride keeps him from being honest with God. In the end, Jesus says, it is the tax collector who comes away justified because of his humility. In the Old Testament, Israel's first king, Saul, refuses to obey God to destroy the plunder from a defeated foe, and when Samuel confronts him about it, Saul says his decision is because he wanted to offer those things to God. These are just two examples in the Bible in which people spin their disobedience and try to make it sound like righteousness before God. None of us are above that, so we need to make sure our hearts are genuinely humble before the Lord.

The author and theologian Francois Fenelon said, "Sometimes we find the most surprising faults in otherwise good people. But we must not be surprised. It is best to let these faults alone and let God deal with them in His time. If we deal with them, we shall end up pulling up the wheat with the tares. I have found that God leaves, even in the most spiritual people, certain weaknesses which seem to be entirely out of place. This is true of us all. And all of us need to be quick to recognize our own imperfection, letting God deal with them. As for you, labor to be patient with the weaknesses of other people. You know from experience how bitterly it hurts to be corrected. So work hard to make it less bitter for others" (Francois Fenelon, *Let Go,* Whitaker House, 1973, pp. 50, 51). I too have found surprising and seemingly out-of-place weaknesses in otherwise very godly people . . . but then, I still see some surprising weaknesses in myself. These are areas, if

> "I have found that God leaves, even in the most spiritual people, certain weaknesses which seem to be entirely out of place. This is true of us all."
> –Francois Fenelon

we are willing to humble ourselves, that cause us to lean into God's grace in our own broken lives and remind us to extend God's grace to the broken people around us. When we find ourselves negative and critical of others, or quick to judge, we are not walking in humility with God. We need to become more acquainted with our own shortcomings, and honest about those, so we can develop humility.

Sometimes our self-protection hinders us from self-disclosure with God and others. In our relationship with God, often it comes down to taking offense at God. We are hurt by something God has allowed in our lives or some prayer God hasn't answered, and our hurt diminishes our trust in God and causes us to build up walls of self-protection. We must let go of our offense to draw near to God. I made a covenant with God many years ago that I would never take offense with Him again. When I took offense at God, I was withdrawing my heart from Him because I was hurt; I was asking God to prove His goodness to me again. But I decided that God had proven His goodness to me on the cross, and by redeeming hard situations to help me know and be like Jesus, and that I needed to trust Him no matter what. He had earned trust; now I needed to put my childish way of taking offense behind me and trust God with the trust He deserved. That decision greatly enhanced my intimacy with God. We cannot draw near to someone we do not trust. We must work through our offenses with God.

> We cannot draw near to someone we do not trust. We must work through our offenses with God.

87

We can also be hindered in our self-disclosure with God because we have stopped growing. Similar to our relationship with other people, if I have stopped learning new things about myself, I am going to be telling the same old story, and I am not going to grow deeper. Are you growing? Are you discovering new things about yourself? What have you discovered about yourself lately that you need to process with God? In my relationship with God, for example, recently I have been processing the speed of my life. I tend to schedule things tightly because of my desire to accomplish things and my desire to get back from conferences to be with my family. But the tight scheduling sometimes causes me to miss out on divine appointments. I want to be a witness for Christ wherever I go, and I pray often for divine appointments. This morning I was out getting a coffee, and a woman asked me a question. I answered her politely, but I realized that if I were not in a hurry to get home because I wanted to write, I likely could have had a meaningful conversation with her. I repented, and I am committed to slowing down to capture the divine appointments God has for me.

Practices for Self-Disclosure

Let me suggest some practices that can aid us in self-disclosure. If I am going to discover new things about God, I must develop a consistent, effective spiritual rhythm. I have written often about developing a spiritual rhythm in my books, so you can read *Spiritual Authority, The Soul Care Leader*, or *River Dwellers* if you want to go deeper with this. I will say just three things about it here.

First, we need to spend time with God if we are going to develop intimacy. My time with God has been a non-negotiable part of my calendar for nearly four decades. That commitment has been essential to developing intimacy with God. I have given Him space to reveal Himself to me. "And without faith it is impossible to please God, because anyone who comes to him must believe that he exists and that he rewards those who earnestly seek him" (Hebrews 11:6). That's a conditional promise; we must believe that God rewards the faith-filled who earnestly seek Him. He will reward them with His presence, with new revelation about ourselves and Himself, and with deeper connection with Him.

Second, keep your time with God fresh. It is easy for your routine to become a rut. All too often our spiritual practices become mundane and boring. We do the same practices, we pray the same words, we sing the same songs, and we fall into a religious rut. We aren't discovering new things about God or ourselves; we're going through the motions. One of the things I've discovered about engaging in spiritual disciplines for a lifetime is that, to keep it fresh, I have to change my rhythm frequently: change holds the master key. My grandmother used to change around her furniture all the time. She owned an antique shop, and she used to move furniture out of the antique shop and into her house, and out of her house and into the antique shop. I used to joke with her that everything in the house except my grandfather had a price tag on it! She would move entire rooms in the house. One time I came to see her, and she had changed

> Keep your time with God fresh. It is easy for your routine to become a rut.

her entire living quarters for my aunt's living quarters—they were living in a duplex, and they swapped living areas! She liked to change things around; it made things new and fresh. It's the same in our relationship with God. We have to keep things new and fresh if we are going to aid our journey toward discovering new things about ourselves and God.

I change spiritual practices around like my grandmother changed her furniture. I change Bibles, change the translation I am reading, and change my approach to Scripture. I pray Scripture, meditate on Scripture, study Scripture, read Scripture, and engage with the Bible in different ways. When my approach gets a little tired, I change it up. The key question I ask myself and others: is your rhythm working? If not, change it. You know the definition of insanity: doing the same thing and expecting different results. If it isn't working, ask God what to do differently, and change your rhythm.

> The key question I ask myself and others: is your rhythm working? If not, change it.

Third, sacrifice has been a vital part of my self-discovery journey. Fasting, watching, and retreating are my three favorite sacrificial practices. When I want to draw near to God I sacrifice food, sleep (I get up in the night to pray), or time (I go away for a retreat). When I feel my relationship with God has plateaued, I immediately pursue a sacrificial spiritual act. I set aside a day to spend alone with God, and I fast during the retreat day. These sacrificial approaches to my intimacy with God have been a huge help. Often on these retreat days I have discovered something that was hindering my spiritual growth: God shined light into my soul, and this led to self-discovery, self-disclosure, and greater intimacy with God. Often on these retreat days God has revealed something new to me about Himself, some facet of his love or faithfulness or holiness that I have never seen before. And in these discoveries, I have drawn nearer to God. Nothing has helped my spiritual journey into intimacy more than the combination of daily time with God and sacrificial pursuit of God's presence. If you aren't doing that currently, I cannot urge you strongly enough to begin immediately.

One of the practices that greatly helps the journey toward self-discovery is to make sure our heart is prepared to receive from the Lord. Don't just do religious activity because that is what you are supposed to do; prepare your heart to meet with God. I believe the greatest hindrance to our next level of intimacy with God is our unprocessed soul issues. Processing these issues opens new chambers of the heart where we can experience God in deeper ways. This is why, as I talked about in *The Soul Care Leader,* I process my negative emotions every day. My negative emotions are the earliest indicator that something is off in my soul. When I am in step with the Spirit, I experience love, joy, and peace (Galatians 5:22). When I'm out of step with the Spirit, I experience annoyance, anger, irritation, and anxiety (or other similar negative emotions). So every day I process my negative emotions, and this leads me to discover things that are "off" in my soul and allows me to do the heart work of getting into alignment with the Lord.

I also take time every day to make sure my sin is confessed before God so it isn't hindering my intimacy. And I take time to make sure my heart is slowed down, not in a hurry, and ready to linger with and receive from the Lord; this is one of the reasons I spend time in silence nearly every day. I want to do my part to make sure I have "ears to hear and eyes to see" and a heart to receive everything the Lord has for me. It was often the religious people in the New Testament who resisted Jesus; they did all the right activities, but their hearts were not prepared to receive.

Another practice that has helped me to grow in my self-disclosure with God has been spiritual reading. When Jen and I hit the marriage snag in our early years of marriage, I read more than fifty books on heart and soul topics. Those books helped me uncover all kinds of brokenness issues, coping mechanisms, driving motivations for sinful or dysfunctional behaviors, and a wide variety of things that were underneath the surface behaviors. As I discovered those things, I processed them with God first. I read books that brought enlightenment, and then I processed with God, and He revealed more to me. It took me deeper in intimacy with God. I also processed what I was reading and discovering with Jen, and that took us deeper as well. Wrestling with what I was discovering through reading with the Lord took me deeper into those topics and allowed God to show me more things about myself, drawing me deeper still.

I love reading the ancients. If you have read any of my other books, you know that one of my favorite ancient writers is Fenelon (mentioned earlier in this chapter), and my favorite book of his is *Let Go.* I have read *Let Go* more than fifty times because it has helped me discover nuances and facets of my self-life. The more I've discovered and processed with the Lord, the freer I have become, and the more it has drawn me into intimacy with Him. I like reading people who have such depth that I can read them over and over and continue to discover new things about me and God.

> In our journey toward self-discovery we must fight our base instinct to resist.

Finally, in our journey toward self-discovery we must fight our base instinct to resist. Often we hit walls of resistance and, rather than figure them out, we let them dictate our path, and our resistance keeps us from intimacy. When I began the journey of self-discovery because of marriage pain, I found myself often running into the wall of resistance. I was resistant to read certain books because, in my mind, they were psychobabble. I felt some resistance to certain parts of a Leanne Payne Conference because it was outside my experience. Sometimes people come to Soul Care Conferences, and they feel resistance because I am challenging their worldview, or because of demonic issues. I was once leading a Soul Care Conference where a participant was arguing with me over all kinds of things that were not primary issues. And I finally said to the man, "You are arguing because you have demons." He laughed because he thought I was kidding, but when Saturday came and we did the group test, much to his surprise (though not to mine), he had demons. We got him free, in Jesus' name, and he no longer felt that resistance inside. Whether resistance is human or demonic, we must be careful not to allow it to keep us from self-discovery and intimacy.

Sadly, it is often my pride that causes me to resist. I tell the story at Soul Care Conferences that when I went to Leanne Payne, I made a commitment to the Lord that I would fight against my resistance and remain open to Him. I knew this stuff was new to me. It was outside of my theological and experiential boxes at times, both of which made me naturally resistant, though not necessarily right. I was aware that my resistance could keep me from freedom, so I determined to stay open before God. I was also feeling some resistance because I had built up years of defense mechanisms to protect me from hurt—but they also shielded me from self-awareness and ultimately from healing. So when someone started pushing against those walls of self-protection, my instinct was to double down and reinforce the walls. I was resistant to the language; Payne was more psychological than theological in her training, so she used the language of psychology more than I was comfortable with at the time. But I knew I was broken, and my marriage was in trouble, and that made me realize I needed help. Desperation is often the platform of breakthrough because it makes us humble enough to listen and be open to new solutions.

The first night of the conference one of Leanne's colleagues was speaking on separation anxiety, and immediately I could feel my resistance pushing back. I wanted to fight against the language, the concept, and the teaching. But I had made the commitment to God that I would fight against my resistance, so I said to Him, "I can feel the resistance beginning, but I don't want to resist. I want to stay open, so show me what you need me to learn. I am broken, and I am here to receive whatever you have for me, Lord." A little while later during that talk I started feeling anxiety intensifying within me. For the rest of the week, every time I entered the sanctuary I felt anxiety, and every time I left it, it would peter out. I knew the Lord was helping me overcome my resistance that was keeping me from self-discovery, self-disclosure, healing, and new levels of intimacy. My commitment to stay open and humble before the Lord was critically important to the healing I later received. It changed my life. But if I had not remained open, I never would have discovered what I needed to find that led to breakthroughs. When you feel resistance, don't justify it, go after it. What is underneath that resistance, really? Get to the heart and soul issues; don't keep them in the intellectual realm. What is it that is bothering you so deeply?

> If I had not remained open, I never would have discovered what I needed to find that led to breakthroughs. When you feel resistance, don't justify it, go after it.

Vulnerability

We must shift from transparency to vulnerability if we are going to go deep with God. The key to shifting to vulnerability is authentic faith. I am entrusting myself to God. There is a big difference between passive faith and active faith. With passive faith I believe the right things and say the right things, but I am not deeply trusting God. I have the right religious phrases, but my heart isn't resting in a deep trust. I still worry, I am still afraid, I still seek to control outcomes, I still get angry and offended that God isn't doing what I want. Often my faith is too shallow to process deeply with God and trust Him to redeem life's most difficult circumstances. I haven't really surrendered. This kind of passive faith is typical of religion, but it is not the active trust the Bible calls us to.

Active trust in God calls us to be vulnerable. We must learn how to rely on God, depend on Him, and count on Him. We trust Him and hold on for His promises even when God doesn't deliver when we think He should or as we think He should. We process through the heartache, disappointment, and pain. Unprocessed pain diminishes authentic active faith, and we end up with a passive religious faith; we are left with the right religious words without the right heart connection.

This kind of active faith requires us to wrestle with God. Passive faith can be a *que sera, sera* attitude: "whatever will happen, will happen; there is nothing I can do." But this isn't the faith I see honored by God in the Scriptures. Noah was told to preach a message of repentance and to build an ark in a desert because a flood was coming. He preached for a long time about an impending flood that simply didn't come—year after year. That is a persistent faith that is action-oriented and perseveres through persecution; there was nothing passive about it. He is commended by God because of this faith. Abraham believed God for a promised land that he would inherit, and he picked up and left his homeland to follow God into a foreign place where he had not been; he didn't know where he was going! God just told him to go, and he went. That's not passive faith; that is active, action-oriented, gut-wrenching trust that God will deliver on His promises. Abraham bet his future on God's faithfulness. Then Abraham believed the promise that he would have a baby when he was 75 years old and his wife 65! These two old-timers were told they would become the spiritual parents of a great nation that would bless the entire world. And against all human reason, they believed. But the baby didn't come . . . for twenty-five years. They waited. They wobbled. They struggled. They sought human means to bring about God's promises. But they held on and, in the end, God delivered. "And so from this one man, and he as good as dead, came descendants as numerous as the stars in the sky and as countless as the sand on the seashore" (Hebrews 11:12).

Here is the painful part of this kind of trusting: we are living for another realm, we are merely aliens in this world, passing through; our true citizenship is in another place. So, all our promises are only partially fulfilled here on earth. "All these people were still living by faith when they died. They did not receive the things promised; they only saw them and welcomed them from a distance, admitting that they were foreigners and strangers on earth. People who say such things show that they are looking for a country of their own. If they had been thinking of the country they had left, they would have had opportunity to return. Instead, they were longing for a better country—a heavenly one. Therefore, God is not ashamed to be called their God, for he has prepared a city for them" (Hebrews 11:13-16).

That's what true faith looks like. It looks like holding on in spite of a myriad of disappointments and setbacks. It looks like believing God for the impossible promise and looking like a fool in people's eyes. It looks like trusting God when only part of the promise is fulfilled, and not taking offense because we realize that some of our promises are only going to be realized in Heaven. It is trusting that the eternal, invisible realm is more real and lasting than the temporal, material realm. It is believing that an invisible God is establishing an eternal spiritual kingdom that is more real and beneficial than this world that we experience with our senses. True faith looks like processing all the disappointment and heartache so the weary flame of your faith isn't snuffed out by offense against God. True faith is identifying with the God of the cross and being certain of His goodness because, in love, He hung on a tree. True faith is holding on to the goodness of God when everything in this temporal world is going wrong, and doing so because you believe the King of Heaven will make everything right in eternity.

It is easier to give up, to resign our hearts to a fatalistic faith—"whatever will be, will be." It is easier to settle for the good things that this life offers and not hold on to the promises of God that are fraught with brokenhearted hopefulness. It is easier to not trust God and actively hold on to the promises He gives because the pathway to obtain those promises are often filled with as many heart-wrenching defeats as they are soul-stirring victories.

We all have to learn how to rely on God, and most often we learn it through well-processed pain. James said, "Consider it pure joy, my brothers and sisters, whenever you face trials of many kinds, because you know that the testing of your faith produces perseverance. Let perseverance finish its work so that you maybe be mature and complete, not lacking anything" (James 1:2-4). Our faith must be tested; we must persevere through the testing to allow our faith to become mature and complete. Testing our faith is essential for maturity.

I learned to rely on God's love when we reached the point, during the marriage crisis in our early years, that my wife didn't love me anymore. I had to develop a faith that went beyond a declaration of who I was in Christ; I had to develop a faith that learned how to "know and rely on the love God has for us" (1 John 4:16). I learned to rely on God's love with active trust; I learned to entrust myself to God's love when Jen didn't love me anymore and there were no guaranteed outcomes. Through developing active faith I experienced the sufficiency of Jesus' love.

I discovered how to trust God actively when we were in that marriage crisis, and the Lord said to me, "I want you to thank me for this marriage pain." I replied, "Lord, I am grateful for many things, even in the midst of this hard season, but this marriage pain isn't one of the things I am grateful for." I heard the inner voice of God say, "One day you will be more grateful for this than almost anything that comes into your life. But it won't take faith to be grateful once I have redeemed this crisis. It only takes faith to give thanks that I will redeem it before I have done so." In faith, I started giving God thanks before I could see the outcome. These are the decisions we have to make if faith is going to shift from a passive religious faith to a deep, active trust in God. I gave thanks every day that God *would* (future tense) redeem that marriage crisis. I didn't know if we would make it, but I knew God told me to give thanks because He could redeem the pain (James 1; Romans 8). So I gave thanks, and God redeemed that marriage crisis to teach me the principles that led me to greater health and wholeness and eventually led me to write *Soul Care*. It has literally changed hundreds of thousands of people's lives around the world. And now it is easy to give thanks.

Hindrances to Vulnerability

What are some of the hindrances to trusting God like this? Sometimes it's hard for us to shift from a passive religious faith to an active faith because we are afraid to trust God in this way. We are afraid we will be hurt; we are afraid we will be disappointed. We are afraid God won't come through, and if God doesn't come through, where else do we have to turn? We are afraid to be authentically vulnerable because it is painful; we feel so weak and exposed. Not everything is going to work out in this world, so entrusting ourselves to God inevitably will lead to some heartache, and this can be scary for us. This is why the Bible says, and frequently: "Do not be afraid." God knew our fear would threaten to squelch our active trust.

One of the hindrances to active faith is unprocessed pain. The problem with unprocessed pain is it often leads us to close our hearts in a self-protective maneuver to avoid more pain. We use anger and numbing as a shield to insulate ourselves from the disappointment of unfulfilled promises and unanswered prayers. But this closing of our hearts results in taking offense at God, and we build up walls around our heart that shut God out. We move to transparency without vulnerability. Again, this is why I process my negative emotions every day, and it is why I made a covenant with God that I would never again take offense at Him. I had to get past this if I was going to develop a deep, active trust in the Lord.

Another hindrance to true trust is our selfish, unsurrendered heart. Sometimes I simply want my own way, and I am unwilling to surrender to the Lord. I trust God . . . as long as God does what I want Him to do. But that isn't real faith; that is a manipulative, self-centered religious appeal to God. And if He doesn't deliver, we turn our back, harden our heart, and pull away. We are using God to get what we want, and if He doesn't come through, we take offense. When Jen and I went through our marriage crisis, I had to surrender Jen, my marriage, and my deepest desires to God. I would follow Jesus and love Jen even if she never loved me again, even if she left me.

Years later I was holding on to the promises of God for revival, and I was preaching revival as the Lord told me to do. But revival wasn't coming. In fact, instead, I went through a long season of attacks. I was weary and disappointed. I wanted to quit every day. One day I read Hebrews 11 and knew I needed to surrender. I needed to hold on for the promise of God—but not be disappointed if it didn't come during my lifetime. I needed to preach revival and pray for revival even if it never happened during my life, even if I was fighting for a promise for a future generation. I surrendered that day and told the Lord I would preach on and fight for revival until I died, even if I never saw it. It was shortly after I surrendered that I made the covenant never to take offense at God again. Not long after, I came out of a dark night of the soul and began to experience a dramatic increase in God's power. If we are going to develop true faith, we need to actively trust God even when things don't go our way.

> Active trust means I trust God for the impossible promises He speaks of in Scripture, and I refuse to take offense when I am battling for those promises without seeing any progres.

We need to give up our selfish ways and surrender to God. Active trust means I trust God for the impossible promises He speaks of in Scripture, and I refuse to take offense when I am battling for those promises without seeing any progress, even if it lasts for a season in my life. It isn't easy to develop this kind of active trust; this is why we so often opt for passive faith or even unbelief.

Practices for Vulnerability

Here are some practices I have engaged in that have helped me stay open and vulnerable before the Lord. First, I have chosen to hold on to the promises of God. I have chosen to trust God actively for the things He has told me in His Word and through His Holy Spirit. I believe everything we receive directly from the Holy Spirit must be tested humbly before the Lord. We must test it with Scripture. If it disagrees with Scripture, then it isn't from the Lord. It is also useful to test these things we receive from the Lord with other believers who hear God's voice consistently and accurately. But after I have tested a promise from the Lord, I hold on to it with immovable resolve. This does expose my heart and motives before the Lord. It also makes me vulnerable before the Lord, because sometimes I am battling for a promise, but I cannot see any progress being made. It brings to light all my doubts, distrust, selfishness, and other dark and weak places. In my book *The Soul Care Leader*, I wrote:

> I think one of the most difficult things in my walk with God has been taking the promises of God seriously. So often there is a painful gap between the magnitude of God's promises that are found in His Word or through direct revelation and the reality of my experience. We have several options we can choose. First, we can let go of the promises of God, stop pursuing them, and settle for a life that is humanly possible to achieve but well beneath our potential as Christ followers. Many people land here, but for me it is a life not worth living. I have to take God seriously and close the gap between what God says and my actual experience. Second, we can hold on to the promises and live in

denial that the gap exists. If we do this, we will become shallow religious people with trite religious phrases and significant gaps in our soul. Third, we can hold on to the promises of God and wrestle with the gaps, the disappointments, the delays, and the partially fulfilled promises—and struggle to develop a deep, authentic faith.

This last one is what I have chosen, and I have to say it has been the harder path. It has set me up for more disappointments and more failures, more sadness and more grief, more heartache and more pain, more wrestling with God and more difficult questions. But I also have to say it has brought me closer to God; I have seen more of what God can do, and I've died to self in a greater way because of this path. I have seen more miracles, experienced more of God's power, touched more of God's presence, and witnessed more of God's breakthroughs because of this choice. It has left me scarred by grief and marked by the presence of God. If I had to do life over, I would take this path again (*The Soul Care Leader*, pp. 10, 11).

Second, I process my disappointments, heartaches, and negative emotions with the Lord. As I said, I process these emotions every day; it has become part of my daily routine so they will not accumulate in my soul. Sometimes it takes me a while to get to the true underlying emotion and root cause. Sometimes it takes me a while to grieve my losses and heartaches and work through an emotion like sadness. So I keep processing until love, joy, and peace emerge again in my soul; this is the fruit of the Spirit. When I am feeling fear, anxiety, sadness, anger, irritation, aggravation, annoyance, and the like, I know I have more processing to do. So I keep digging; I keep asking God to show me if there is something underneath that negative emotion, and I keep processing until love, joy, and peace resurface in my soul. (I've covered this in other books, like *River Dwellers* and *The Soul Care Leader*, so you can refer to those if you are looking for more help with processing.) We cannot allow our unprocessed negative emotions to accumulate in our souls without numbing our hearts to God.

Third, I have resolved to persevere in my life. I will persevere through whatever comes my way without letting go of God, without letting go of active faith, and without quitting my assignments from God. When I went through the marriage crisis, I wanted to quit ministry nearly every day, and sometimes I wanted to quit on marriage because it was so painful. But I told the Lord I would not quit; I resolved to persevere. Perseverance resulted in maturity. When I went through the prolonged season of attacks in ministry because I was preaching on revival, I wanted to quit nearly every day. But the Lord kept saying, "Put your hand to the plow and do not look back." So I persevered with steely resolve. I told the Lord I would not quit pastoring the church until He released me. That perseverance resulted in maturity and authority like I had never experienced before. And I didn't quit until God released me. When COVID came and it robbed me of all the joys of ministry (the human interactions, the stories, the tears, the power of God on visible display) and filled my heart with sadness, I wanted to quit again. But I persevered. The God who redeemed the marriage crisis and the God who redeemed the ministry crisis would redeem the pandemic crisis. And He has. It created a much deeper, more impactful reach than we ever had before because we were forced to go to livestreams, and this caused me to sink deeper roots in my heavenly citizenship.

Fourth, I have actively chosen to remember my history with God. This has been a faith-building exercise for me. Whenever I enter into a new crisis, I review my history with God. I review God's history with me, with my family, and with His people throughout the Scriptures. I remind myself that this is who Jesus is and this is what Jesus does. He is the same yesterday, today, and forever (Hebrews 13:8). He has not changed. Reviewing my history with God reminds of who God is, of God's faithfulness, and that God has delivered in the past, and this strengthens my grip on God's goodness to deliver again in the present. Hardship has a way of weakening our grasp on the goodness of God. Thanksgiving over God's faithful dealings with us in our past strengthens our grip on God's goodness to carry us through our present struggles. I have to say that, having survived some significant, long-standing, painful events in my past, and having seen God deliver me and redeem them in my life, has greatly helped me develop an active trust in Him. But I have done my part too. I have persevered through those crises—the marriage pain, the ministry pain, and the like. I obeyed God and gave thanks when it made no sense; I intentionally held on to the promises of God

> Hardship has a way of weakening our grasp on the goodness of God. Thanksgiving over God's faithful dealings with us in our past strengthens our grip on God's goodness to carry us through our present struggles.

and reviewed my history with God to strengthen my faith. I processed my negative emotions so I would not take offense at God. Doing those things consistently has been instrumental in the cultivation of a deep, active trust in Him. I didn't sit by passively waiting for God to do my part.

Fifth, I have chosen to remember the cross and eternity in the midst of difficulty and pain. In my book *The Tenderness of Jesus,* I write about how we must view life's difficulties through the lens of the cross and the lens of eternity. The cross reminds us that God is with us and God is for us. Jesus didn't stand aloof from our pain and suffering; He entered into our human experience, and He suffered with us and for us. This continually reminds us that God cares. We may not understand why something happens in our life, but we know that God cares because of the cross. We must constantly look at our broken, painful experiences in life through the lens of the cross to restore our active faith in the goodness of God. We must also look through the lens of eternity. Not everything will work out on earth: not every battle will be won, not every soul will be saved, not every sickness will be cured, not every addict will get free, not every problem will be resolved, not every heartache will be healed, and not every promise will be fully experienced. We will limp through portions of this life because we live in a world that is impacted by evil. Therefore, we will fight for things in the name of God, with prayer and fasting and the tools of the kingdom, and yet we will not see the victory come in all matters. Not on earth. But Heaven will resolve all earth's problems and fulfill all God's promises. Heaven is God's final answer to evil. In Heaven evil will be eradicated, sin will be eliminated, and all the effects of sin will be exterminated. Goodness, justice, and mercy will rule without any interference or challenge. You cannot make sense of a life tainted by sin without the lens of eternity. So when I'm struggling with hardships, I view them through the lens of the cross and the lens of eternity to give me a more accurate perspective. It strengthens my weak and wobbly faith and helps me surrender to a God who can be trusted because He is the God of the cross and the King of Heaven.

Self-Control

If we are going to develop intimacy with God, we must grow in holiness, and this involves self-control. Example: if a husband is calling his wife names, and she confronts him and he admits it is wrong, but he continues to do it, they are not going to develop intimacy. He must not simply admit that he is wrong, he must change. If he says he doesn't want to call her names anymore but keeps doing it, continually makes excuses for his behavior, and gives reasons for why he keeps doing it, she is not going to trust him. Trust is the foundation of an intimate relationship. Without repentance, without changing our wrongful behaviors, trust cannot be re-established, and intimacy is hampered.

We have to practice self-control if we are going to change. We must choose to say no to self, yes to God, and obey Jesus. Jesus said (Matthew 5:8), "Blessed are the pure in heart, for they will see God." Notice that Jesus indicates our holiness needs to go beyond behaviors; it needs to be a purity of heart. Our motives need to be right before God, as well as our actions. The Pharisees often did the right things, but their motives were impure. They prayed, fasted, and engaged in sacrificial acts, but their true motives were to be noticed and receive the applause of people. They were motivated by pride. That cannot be a path to create intimacy with God. It is impossible to be holy before the Lord without congruence. What we say, and what we do, and why we do it, must all be in alignment with Jesus. This requires ruthless honesty, authentic humility, and personal responsibility.

We must be willing to see our heart motivations, and when they are impure, we must be willing to repent if we are going to walk in holiness before the Lord. Humility is the one indispensable characteristic necessary to begin to change.

> This requires ruthless honesty, authentic humility, and personal responsibility. We must be willing to see our heart motivations, and when they are impure, we must be willing to repent.

The problem is that the motivations of our heart are so subtle, and the human capacity for self-deception is nearly endless. Let me give an example. One day early in my ministry, I brought an issue to our church board that I wanted the board members to know about. I wasn't looking for them to vote on it or give feedback; I was just looking to inform them of the direction the staff and I were taking. But they labored over the issue for two hours. I was frustrated because I wanted to get to other issues on the agenda, and this issue seemed so clear and so minor to me. I came home and was complaining to Jen about it when I heard the Lord interrupt me. He called me to get alone with Him, and when I did He said, "You were right about the decision you wanted to make, but your attitude was so bad I couldn't use you." The Lord went on to reveal that I had come into the board meeting knowing what I wanted to do rather than seeking to discern the mind of Christ. And then I held tightly to my ideas rather than humbly listening to feedback. I began to make it about winning and losing rather than discovering the mind of Christ. I sensed Jesus saying to me that the number one job of a spiritual leader is to find the mind of Christ and do it. But I wasn't seeking the mind of Christ; rather, I had already made up my mind and was fighting for what I wanted. I went back and apologized to the board and made a commitment to seek the mind of Christ on all issues and to hold more loosely to my ideas.

Hebrews 12:14 says, "Make every effort to live in peace with everyone and to be holy; without holiness no one will see the Lord." Again, the biblical writer reinforces the importance of holiness and intimacy. I think there is a sense in which this passage has an eschatological meaning—that is, no one is going to get to Heaven without the righteousness of Jesus imparted to them. Therefore, each person must repent of their sin and put their faith in Christ for forgiveness to make them acceptable before God. But I also believe there is a relational intimacy truth being revealed here: we cannot draw near to God without growing in holiness. Our unholy behaviors, thoughts, and motives become barriers to our journey toward deep intimacy with Jesus. Notice that this passage links our holiness with our peaceful relationships with other people. Jesus told us that the most important things are to love God and love people. The biblical idea is that we cannot really love God if we are not loving people. The greatest indicator that I am drawing nearer to God is the fact that I am loving God and people better. Holiness begins with love.

Once again, the Pharisees totally missed this. They thought holiness began with good doctrine and right behaviors. They prayed, fasted, tithed, went to synagogue, and didn't do the things the tax collectors were doing. But they neglected mercy, compassion, and love. They looked down on people, judged others, and thought of themselves as better than others. You cannot be holy if you are not loving, no matter what religious activities you are doing. As a matter of fact, if you are engaging in many religious activities but are not growing in love, you are becoming more religious and less like Jesus. So this is a great place to begin examining our heart: are we more loving this year than we were a year ago? Do we love God more? Is Jesus our first love and primary obsession? Do we love people more? When I am increasingly annoyed, aggravated, irritated, and angry, that is not the fruit of the Spirit. When I am yielding my life to Jesus moment by moment, and walking in the light with God, I inevitably become more loving. When I am not becoming more loving, I am not yielding my life to Jesus, and I am not walking in the light with God. I am fooling myself. Something is off in my heart and soul.

We have been talking about holiness. Let's sum up some of what holiness looks like. Holiness begins with love; we love God and love people. Holiness is a congruence between what we do, what we think, and why we do what we do. We have good thinking, good actions, and good motives. Holiness means we represent Jesus well to people. When people are with us, are they attracted to Jesus? Holiness means that we know and become like Jesus; we are drawing near to Him and living more like Him. Jesus is holy, so holiness is to become like Jesus and represent Him well in every human interaction and every private motivation. When we blow it—and we certainly will—to be holy means we humble ourselves before God and others, admit our wrongdoing, and repent. We are honest with God and others. We cannot be humble without honesty; we cannot be holy without humility. Holiness means we have contrite hearts. God doesn't expect perfection from us, but He does expect contrition.

We have responsibility in the process of growing to become more like Jesus. We cannot be passive. We must engage in responsible behaviors and self-control. I want to give you a picture of New Testament sanctification (the process of becoming holy, like Jesus). There is a difference between Old Testament sanctification and New Testament sanctification. In the Old Testament, when the clean came in contact with the unclean, the clean became defiled. So when a person touched a leper or a dead body, they became defiled; they were now "unclean." But in the New Testament, when the clean touches the unclean, the unclean becomes clean! (I am indebted to my friend Ron Walborn for this insight.) God's New Testament strategy for your holiness development is to deposit His Holy Spirit directly into the middle of your messy life. In Luke 11:13, Jesus says, "If you then, though you are evil, know how to give good gifts to your children, how much more will your Father in heaven give the Holy Spirit to those who ask him!" Jesus calls us evil, but He promises us that the Father will give the Holy Spirit to us if we ask, because we cannot clean ourselves up by our human effort; we need God's presence and power.

When you came to faith in Christ, you didn't stop sinning. 1 John 1 makes it clear that we all still sin, and if we say we don't we are lying and make God out to be a liar. When you came to faith in Christ, it didn't heal all your heartache and brokenness. You still have child-hood wounds and pain from your past. There is still sin, dysfunction, and pain within us. Jesus didn't make us clean ourselves up to become acceptable to Him before He would give us His Holy Spirit. In the New Testament, Jesus' strategy for making us like Him is to give us

> He puts His Spirit right into the hot mess of our heart and soul! He deposits His Spirit in there with all our sin, dysfunction, and pain.

the Holy Spirit, and He puts His Spirit right into the hot mess of our heart and soul! He deposits His Spirit in there with all our sin, dysfunction, and pain. Our job is not to change ourselves but to yield ourselves to the Spirit for life change. Our job is not to hide or cover our sin and pain but to humbly bring it into the light where God can address it. Our job is to cooperate with the Spirit for empowered holy living. We cannot become holy by sheer willpower. But neither can we become holy by being passive and waiting around for God to do our part. We have a part to play. We must learn to yield ourselves to the Spirit; we must learn how to walk "in step" with the Holy Spirit, as Paul says, or to "walk in the light" with God and others, as John says.

Paul says that part of the fruit of the Spirit is self-control (Galatians 5:23). The Holy Spirit is essential to the process of self-control. But we have to take responsibility for our lives if we are going to become mature. Let's talk about some hindrances and some helps to the process of self-control and life change.

Hindrances to Self-Control

The first hindrance to self-control is pride. If we are proud, we will be unwilling to admit that we are wrong, unwilling to admit that we need to change, and unwilling to listen to other people when they point out our flaws. Proud people are not teachable, and pride becomes a barrier to transformation. The only way for a proud person to grow is to humble himself or herself before God and others. When Jen and I hit our marriage snag early on, as we started having conversations about our marriage, Jen gave me feedback on things I was doing to hurt her. Each time she pointed something out, I defended myself. My defensiveness came from pride and insecurity, and it blocked me from receiving what I needed to hear so I could change. The Lord revealed to me that only insecure people are defensive and that my defensiveness was blocking me from receiving the light He was offering to help me grow. I had to humble myself before the Lord and stop defending myself with Jen before I could receive truth and change. My pride made me incapable of taking responsibility and moving forward with life change. Humility was the only remedy.

When you are quick to defend yourself and slow to admit wrongdoing, quick to shift blame and slow to take responsibility, quick to make excuses and slow to receive feedback, quick to flare up in anger and slow to listen, you are inevitably moving in pride that will keep you from life change. The only remedy is to humble yourself before God and others. Otherwise, intimacy will always be elusive to you.

Second, one of the things that often hinders people from taking ownership for their life and moving ahead is a victim mentality. Many people have been victimized in life—they have suffered physical, emotional, and/or sexual abuse. But hear this: though you may have been victimized, you are not a victim. Not in Christ you aren't! Because Christ is in us, and we are in Christ, we can overcome. Often when someone has been victimized, that person feels powerless to change. So it is hard for him to take responsibility for his life. It reduces him to powerless passivity. He may have overpowering emotions and may feel like there is nothing he can do, but there is always hope in Christ because Christ is never powerless. For us to begin to exercise self-control that leads to life change, we must change our mindset. We have to realize that we may have been victimized, but we are not victims because we are in Christ. We are weak, but we are not powerless to change because we are in Christ. We are hurt, but we are not paralyzed to overcome because we are in Christ. Our victimization often leads us to believe the lie that we are powerless to change. So we will not take responsibility for our lives and move ahead until we confront that lie. It leaves us feeling passive, and we catch ourselves thinking, *Why won't God help me?*

Third, sometimes we are hindered from taking life-altering responsibility because of our unaddressed soul issues. There is something from our past that is hindering us from moving ahead in our present. In my book *Soul Care*, I write about seven topics that must be addressed if we are going to experience the transformation Jesus has for us. I have said this for many years now: *Soul Care* is not a book to be read like a novel, and it is not simply a conference to be attended in three days. It is a lifestyle to be adopted. We have to live out these principles, not just take these principles in. One of the reasons I developed an eCourse on Soul Care is to help people live out these principles in their daily lives. This is one of the major problems with religion: we believe the right things, we know the right answers, we can quote the right verses. Therefore, we think we have mastered the material. We show up at a conference, we take notes, and we think, *I've got it*. But that simply is not true. When it comes to identity, for example, the question isn't: "Do you know you are loved by God?" If you grew up going to church, you have heard that message, you know that truth, and you can likely even quote a number of verses to back it up. The right question is: "Are you living like a deeply loved person in all your interactions?" If you know you are loved, but you are still defensive, you are not living like a deeply loved person. If you know you are loved, but you are still too fearful to engage in difficult conversations, you're not living like a deeply loved person. If you know you are loved but are still entertaining negative, critical self-talk, you are not living like a deeply loved person. Your identity hasn't made its way into your daily existence, and that will not produce life change. Some of you have read *Soul Care*, but you haven't done the work. You know the principles, but you have not integrated them into your life. You must do the work of integration. I have explained how to do that in *Soul Care, The Soul Care Leader*, and the Soul Care eCourse. I strongly urge you to go back and work and rework those until you live them.

Practices for Self-Control

Let's talk about practical things we can do to help us to manage life change and exercise the kind of self-control, under the power of the Holy Spirit, that leads to new life patterns.

First, we have to get to the root issues. If we are going to experience authentic life change, we must make sure we are dealing with the issues of the heart and soul, not merely managing behavior. Jesus said to the Pharisees: "Woe to you, teachers of the law and Pharisees, you hypocrites! You clean the outside of the cup and dish, but inside they are full of greed and self-indulgence. Blind Pharisee! First clean the inside of the cup and dish, and then the outside also will be clean" (Matthew 23:25, 26). Jesus also said to the Pharisees, "You brood of vipers, how can you who are evil say anything good? For out of the overflow of the heart the mouth speaks" (Matthew 12:34). We cannot merely address behaviors. We must address the heart if we are going to have breakthroughs that allow us to walk with God in intimacy.

> If we are going to experience authentic life change, we must make sure we are dealing with the issues of the heart and soul, not merely managing behavior.

Too often in the church we worry about cleaning up the outside of the dish. If we clean up filthy language, but we're filled with judgmental, negative, critical attitudes, we are still not holy. If we clean up sexual immorality, but our hearts harbor selfishness and lust, we are still not holy. If we clean up stealing, but our hearts are full of envy and covetousness, we are still not holy. We have to bring the external behaviors as well as the internal motivations to God, and we have to stand in the light with God and others. We have to wrestle with God to discover why we do what we do, and we must bring it all to God for His purification. We have to learn to live a surrendered life in authentic humility so we can begin to walk in the power of the Spirit.

I've had to reflect deeply and often about my motives to make it possible to draw nearer to God. Again, processing my negative emotions often helps me get there. I have wrestled often with the questions: "What's underneath that?" "Why do I do what I do?" "Why do I feel what I feel?" "Why do I think what I think?" I have welcomed the Spirit's light into my inner being so I can walk nearer to God.

I don't want to walk like the Pharisees with a cleaned-up external presentation and yet a messed-up interior heart condition before the Lord. There have been times in my life I have felt my heart rooting against someone. Even though I said the right things, I could feel that I didn't want the person to succeed. I was jealous or envious of them because they were gaining ground in an area in which I wanted to gain ground. Their stock was rising in the people's hearts around me who I wanted to be loved by, or they were succeeding in some area of ministry that I wanted to be successful in. I decided I couldn't be content with simply treating this person well while harboring such envy in my soul. I had to go before the Lord and let Him show me the condition of my heart, the envy that was there, and that I had to repent. On one occasion I actually went to the person and confessed that I wanted him to be liked, just not as liked as I was; I wanted him to be successful, but not as successful as I was. Then I knelt before him and asked him to pray for me. It was a person I had hired on my staff; I couldn't just clean up the outside, I had to go for the condition of the heart. Humbling myself before him resulted in breaking the envy. This is the power of humbling ourselves before the Lord and others—it leads to victory. God empowers humble people. On other occasions, I brought it before the Lord as soon as I felt it, and I simply needed to pray for the other person's success and blessing. That was enough to break free.

I hate seeing these things about my heart. I hate seeing the smallness, pettiness, and selfishness that I sometimes find within my heart and soul. But I hate, even more, not addressing these things and not breaking free from them. The thing that most often prevents us from walking in freedom is our unwillingness to humble ourselves before the Lord and others. If we are going to find freedom, we must get to the heart issues, and that will require humility. Proud people are left with self-empowerment for life change; humble people experience the Spirit's power to overcome.

A second practice that can help us cultivate self-control is to regularly submit ourselves before the Lord. In the story I just told, the reason I went to the staff person and knelt before him was because I could feel myself rooting against him. That is not the person I want to be. Romans 12:15 says, "Rejoice with those who rejoice; mourn with those who mourn." When I was in my twenties, I went to a John Maxwell Conference, and I remember John saying that for many of us it is easier to mourn with those who mourn than it is to rejoice with those who rejoice; this is true because of our insecurity. We feel threatened when other people are successful, fruitful, loved, and financially blessed. We don't naturally rejoice over that. Sadly, if we don't realize our impure motives, we will often spiritualize our distaste for that person: "Their church is growing because they are compromising the gospel." . . . "They are gaining ground financially because they are selfish and greedy." . . . "That person is winning people's affections because they are a people-pleaser."

That Maxwell Conference made me very aware of whenever I was rooting against someone's success. I determined that day that I would not be that kind of small-hearted, small-minded person. I realized it was coming from my insecurity and envy, and I determined to go to God and deal with my motives every time I felt these things in my heart. That day I went to the Lord because I sensed the Lord convicting me that the root of this sin was envy. I had hired this man to bring leadership to people I had been leading, but giving up influence in their life was hard. My heart was envious and protective; I didn't want to lose my position in their hearts. I admitted that before the Lord, and I sensed the Lord telling me to go to the pastor, kneel before him, and ask him to pray for me. It was both hard and freeing. It is always hard to humble ourselves, but freeing when we do so.

> It is always hard to humble ourselves, but freeing when we do so.

I believe the secret to success in life is to find what God wants and do it no matter what it costs. There is no peace without surrender; there is no freedom without death to self. When we feed our self-life, we end up in bondage. It is only when we submit ourselves to the Lord that we discover the freedom that is ours in Christ. The Pharisees would not do that. They would not admit their envy. They would not admit their pride. They would not admit their impure motives that were driving their religious behaviors. They kept reading their Bible, praying, fasting, tithing, and going to church. And they killed Jesus because of their unacknowledged, unresolved heart issues. We have to allow God to reveal to us the motives of our heart, and we must humble ourselves before the Lord or we will end up opposing God and not even knowing it.

We only have three choices we can make in our relationship with God. We can **rebel**: God tells us to do something, and we refuse and do the opposite. God tells us, for example, to forgive, and we say, "I will never forgive that person." That's rebellion. We can **resign**. When we resign, we often feel overpowered by God. He is bigger and stronger, and we can't fight against Him, so we give in. But both resignation and rebellion are rooted in distrust, and neither path leads to victory. We don't believe God is good and that He has our best interest in mind. In rebellion we go our own way. In resignation we sometimes go God's way on the outside, but on the inside we are not motivated by love and trust.

Our third choice is to **surrender**. Only surrender is rooted in trust. Surrender is when we decide to go God's way because we know God is good; we die to self and say yes to God. We may not understand God's way, but we surrender because we trust Him. We say yes to God because He has proven His goodness to us on the cross.

It is often when I say yes to God, surrendering my heart before Him, that I feel the empowerment of the Spirit. I agree to go God's way, and God empowers me to do it. I humble myself before the Lord, and God gives me strength to follow Him. I admit my envy before a staff member and kneel before him for prayer, and God gives me victory over the envy. So often the battle rages when I am struggling to surrender in a privatized religion, but when I finally and truly surrender, I feel free. But remember: you cannot surrender a symptom. If I am struggling with anger, but anger is a symptom of my selfishness, I will not get free from anger until I surrender my selfishness. We have to get to the root issue and surrender that. We have to say yes to God and no to self. That's our part. God will then empower us to change as we humbly surrender to Him.

> Dying to self has meant that I would no longer give myself permission to continue doing what I had been doing.

Third, another thing that has helped me with self-control is dying to self. This has some overlap with the last category—I have to say yes to God (surrender) and no to self (die to self). But I want to give some specific help here. Many times in my life, dying to self has meant that I would no longer give myself permission to continue doing what I had been doing. When Jen and I were working through the marriage crisis in the early days of our relationship, I could no longer give myself permission to give Jen the silent treatment. At one point in my processing, I realized I was giving Jen the silent treatment because I was angry. I wasn't yelling or screaming or name-calling, but I would wall up and shut down. She felt like she was walking on eggshells because of that. When I realized that it was a childish, selfish, self-protective, manipulative behavior, it had to stop. So I stopped giving myself permission to act that way. I told Jen that if I walled up on her with silence, she could call me on it. That was not the man I wanted to be, and it did not represent Jesus well to her. Sometimes people ask me at conferences, "How did you stop using the silent treatment?"

I had to die to self. I had to stop giving myself permission to act in immature, sinful, selfish ways. At the same time, I was dealing with the root issues of my soul; I was processing all the issues of *Soul Care*. I was securing my identity in Christ—not merely with words, but with integration. And all that work was empowering me to say no to self, to die to self, and to refuse to give myself permission to use the silent treatment any longer.

One last thing that has helped me develop self-control—and this has fostered life change—is learning to receive feedback without dismissing it. This was a critical practice for developing humility. I had to stop reacting negatively to feedback. I couldn't do this without doing the identity work, but as I was doing the work of becoming a deeply loved person, I also made a decision to receive feedback and criticism in a constructive way. In the beginning, as I said, I would defend myself. Jen would feel unheard, and the conversation would escalate. We would both get more upset and make no progress. After the Lord told me to stop defending myself because only insecure people defend themselves, I made a decision to stop defending myself! I realized that my defensiveness was keeping me from useful, helpful information that could lead to me to self-awareness and breakthroughs. My insecurity and pride were preventing me from the freedom I longed for, so I decided a new approach to conflicted conversations

> After the Lord told me to stop defending myself because only insecure people defend themselves, I made a decision to stop defending myself!

was needed. I realized I was too upset over the conflict with Jen to respond to the feedback without some process space. I could not receive it dispassionately and simply own my part. So I decided I would listen to what she was saying until I could say it back to her clearly with my own words; then I would take that information to my prayer time alone with God and process it with God. I wouldn't give Jen an immediate response. I just listened and made sure I understood. I knew I couldn't respond to her in the moment without defending myself, but I was able to process that information with God and let Him tell me what was true because I knew He loved me. I processed my pain and hurt with God, I got on the firm foundation of God's love by renewing my mind, and then I asked the Lord, "Out of these things that Jen said to me, what is true about me?" In the security of God's love, I could receive the truth, and then I would go back to Jen and own the things God had told me were true about me.

That new process of learning how to receive criticism without defending myself became critically important to life change. It opened me up to self-awareness, as I wrote earlier, but it also helped me become more self-controlled. I wasn't reacting every time Jen gave me criticism because I had chosen to listen, to die to my right to react and defend myself, and to receive whatever was true and could help me change. The process helped me become more secure and less defensive, more rooted in my identity in Christ and less emotionally volatile, and more open to feedback and less fearful that it invalidated me in some way. I was not only becoming more secure and more deeply loved, I was more open to the truth about myself, and this led me to new levels of freedom in Christ. This carried over into how I received feedback and criticism from people in all walks of life. Listen: many times we receive feedback or criticism that is done all wrong, but some of the information the person is saying with the wrong attitude or wrong tones are actually the right things, things we need to hear. We have to get secure in Christ and have a good process in place to receive that kind of feedback so we can become the people we want to be.

This is the process of becoming intimate with God. We have to grow in **self-discovery, self-disclosure, vulnerability,** and **self-control** so we can draw near to God in ever-deepening ways. The good news for us is that God has no limit. He is infinite, so there is no end to the intimacy we can discover.

The reason Heaven will never be boring is because there will always be new things to discover about God. One million years from now we will still be discovering new facets of God's love. We will say, "I never knew that about God's love!" And a million years later we will still not be able to plumb the limitless depths of the love of God. There is always more to discover. We just have to break free from religion and move into the authentic so we can go deeper with God.

Three

SHIFT

Moving forward, how do we transition from learned religious behaviors to authentic intimacy with God and avoid the pitfalls of religion moving forward? Jesus' disciples came to Him after He taught on the Parable of the Sower and asked:

> "Why do you speak to the people in parables?" He replied, "The knowledge of the secrets of the kingdom of heaven has been given to you, but not to them. Those who have will be given more, and they will have an abundance. As for those who do not have, even what they have will be taken from them. This is why I speak to them in parables: 'Though seeing, they do not see; though hearing, they do not hear or understand.' In them is fulfilled the prophecy of Isaiah: 'You will be ever hearing but never understanding; you will be ever seeing but never perceiving. For this people's heart has become calloused, they hardly hear with their ears, and they have closed their eyes. Otherwise they might see with their eyes, hear with their ears,

understand with their hearts and turn, and I would heal them'" (Matthew 13:10-15).

There is a lot to unpack in this teaching of Jesus since we want to be those who have ears to hear and eyes to see. We want the message of God to land on good soil in our hearts and bear much fruit. I want to talk about some necessary shifts we must undergo if we are going to move to authentic Christian living.

Callous to Contrite

We must shift from callous to contrite hearts, from pride to humility. The reason these people did not have ears to hear or eyes to see was because of the condition of their hearts. The Proverb writer exhorted us, "Above all else, guard your heart, for everything you do flows from it" (Proverbs 4:23). We must fight to keep our hearts soft, broken, humble, contrite before God.

I hear people say all the time that if you say you are humble, then really you are not. But that isn't true. Jesus claimed to be humble ("for I am gentle and humble in heart," Matthew 11:29) and so did the Apostle Paul ("I served the Lord with great humility," Acts 20:19). Claiming to be humble doesn't mean that you are, but claiming to be humble doesn't disqualify you either. *The proof of humility is in how you live.* Words are easy to speak, but does your life demonstrate authentic humility? This is utterly essential for having a heart open to God. Let's review this once more: authentic humility begins with honesty, ends with responsibility, and somewhere in the middle is death to self. Humility is not thinking less of yourself; it is making life less about you. Pride is simply becoming too focused on ourselves. Pride can be about being haughty and boastful, or having lowly shame, or insecurity; pride is simply being self-focused. Authentic humility considers others more important than ourselves (Philippians 2:3). True humility puts Jesus at the center of our lives, not ourselves. We must choose humble actions, especially when our pride is pushing us to put ourselves at the center.

Here are some examples of what this looks like in real time. These examples are not an exhaustive list; they are merely here to help you think about what authentic humility looks like.

Pray for a humble heart. The Lord said, "I will give you a new heart and put a new spirit in you; I will remove from you your heart of stone and give you a heart of flesh" (Ezekiel 36:26). Claim this promise and pray it over your life—especially when you realize you are wrestling with pride and self-focus. I know I am wrestling with pride when I am reluctant to own my part in a conflict. I know I am wrestling with pride when I defend myself. I know I am wrestling with pride when I am selfish. I mention the book *Let Go* by Fenelon often because Fenelon has coached me into death to self better than anyone I know. He has helped me realize when my self-life is greedily grasping for attention. He has helped me see more acutely what it looks like to get wrapped up in self-love and what I need to do to die to self and humble myself before the Lord. So I keep going back to it. I read it slowly and prayerfully because I have struggled with my bias toward self a great deal, and I need all the help I can get to overcome this struggle. Fenelon helps me see when I need to choose humility, and he encourages me to make the right choice.

Receive critical feedback without defensiveness, resentment, or retaliation. This isn't easy. Fenelon wrote, "It is a good sign of real, God-produced humility when we are no longer shocked by the corrections of others, nor by the resistance within." He goes on to say, "If we find ourselves rebelling and getting irritable, we should understand that this irritability under correction is worse than all our other faults put together. And we know that correction is not going to make us any more humble than it finds us. If we have inner resentment at being corrected, that just shows how deeply the correction is needed. In fact, the sting of correction wouldn't be felt at all if the old self were dead. So the more correction hurts, the more we see how necessary it is" (Fenelon, *Let Go,* Whitaker House, pp. 48, 49). Believe me, I understand it is much easier to read these words of Fenelon than it is to live them. Even after years of working on my identity, reading and praying through Fenelon, and seeking God to help me respond with humility, I still sadly discover that my first reaction to criticism is often irritation and defensiveness. I have learned to not act defensively more often than not, and I have learned to get through the offense in a matter of minutes rather than days. But I still often feel defensive because my self-life is not yet fully dead. I long for the day when I can receive criticism with no angst, irritation, aggravation, or defensiveness. In the meantime, though, I want to choose not to defend myself and to humble myself under the hand of correction, even when the person bringing the correction isn't loving. I have to say, making this choice has helped me.

Own everything you can own, even when other people won't own anything. It is a lot easier to own your part if someone else owns their part. If someone comes to me to resolve a conflict and they begin by owning their part of that dispute or disagreement, I am moved by that humble gesture. If they then go on to speak to me about something that I have done to hurt them, it is much easier for me to own my part because of their humble approach. Thus, knowing this, when I have to go to someone else to talk through a conflict, I always try to begin by owning my part. I have discovered that is a gracious lubricant that greases the wheel of conflicted conversations and makes them run more smoothly. But even if the other person comes to attack and is unwilling to own anything, I still need to humble myself before God and own everything I can.

I once had a public situation in which I needed to own my part even though the other person wouldn't own their part. It was a staff member who announced he was going to leave the church because he felt called by God to move on. But I knew he was leaving because he was hurt, and I attempted to resolve the conflict. Finally, he admitted that he was hurt, and we did resolve the conflict, but we had to address the church because the staff member had announced he was called by God to leave. We agreed to stand up before the church and talk about our conflict, we would each own our part, and we would explain how we resolved it. But two days before we were to stand up and give the talk, the man called me and asked, "What was my part?" I knew I was in trouble; I knew he would not own anything when we stood up together on that Sunday. Jen, my wife, asked me privately what I would do if he reneged on our agreement and didn't own his part. I told her I would own my part no matter what. She said to me, "You will look like a fool because this person is going to leave you hanging." I nodded and said to her, "I will look like a fool in everyone's eyes but God's." So I owned my part even though the man owned nothing. The day after he repented, and I forgave him, and we continued to work together.

Be confessional. Be open and honest about your flaws, weaknesses, shortcomings, dysfunction, and sin. As the old expression goes, "Confession is good for the soul." That's because confession is an act of humility. I have found that if I keep my confessions between God and myself alone, this privatized form of religion does not generate a humble heart. But when I bow my stiff neck and humble myself before God to walk in the light with Him and others (1 John 1), it helps the humbling process. I have also found it is not easy to be truly honest with others. I want to skip that part. I want to slip back into privatized religion because it is less damaging to my ego. But pride is damaging to my authentic spiritual experience while humility is essential for true intimacy. I have also discovered that when other people are honest and confessional with me, I am deeply moved. I am drawn to authentic humility and repelled by pride. When people humble themselves, I am moved with grace and compassion, which I know comes from Jesus. God is irresistibly drawn to the contrite of heart, but the proud walk alone.

Finally, if you want to develop authentic humility, **choose to rejoice in your weaknesses, like Paul.** Rejoice in your weaknesses rather than boasting in your strengths. In 2 Corinthians 12 Paul talks about a thorn in the flesh, a messenger of Satan. He asked the Lord to take it away from him three times. But the Lord responded, "My grace is sufficient for you, for my power is made perfect in weakness" (2 Corinthians 12:9). It doesn't really matter what this thorn was. I suspect it was the attacks Paul was under; that is the context in 2 Corinthians 11, and the expression is used in the Old Testament referring to the enemies of Israel. However, what is important here is the Lord's statement to Paul and Paul's response to it. The Lord tells him that His grace is sufficient for Paul's struggle and that His power is made perfect in Paul's weakness. So Paul says, "Therefore I will boast all the more gladly about my weaknesses, so that Christ's power may rest on me. That is why, for Christ's sake, I delight in weaknesses, in insults, in hardships, in persecutions, in difficulties. For when I am weak, then I am strong" (2 Corinthians 12:9, 10). I have read this passage and meditated on it, prayed over it, and pondered over it dozens of times, and I have to say that it still moves me deeply. I am moved by Paul's steely resolve to make life about Jesus, not about himself. I am moved by his willingness to suffer for the sake of Jesus' glory so that Jesus' power can be put on display. I am moved to make life less about me and more about Jesus. I am moved to rejoice in my weaknesses so that Christ may be honored through me. It moves me to want to rejoice in attacks rather than defending myself so Christ's power can be perfected in me. How can we experience the resurrection power of Jesus without the cross?

If we are going to experience an ever-deepening, intimate walk with Jesus that is real and authentic, we must choose humility. We must shift from pride to humility and from a callous heart to a contrite heart. This means making these types of choices consistently over a lifetime. These are the types of choices that beckon the presence of God to us.

Knowledge to Revelation

If we are going to move from religion to authentic intimacy with God, we have to make the shift from knowledge to revelation. The greatest gap in most people's spiritual journey is between that which they know and that which has not yet been made known to them. We have to do our part to close this gap. We cannot create revelation, but we can position ourselves to receive revelation. God wants to make Himself known. In the passage we opened the chapter with, Jesus told His disciples that they had been given the knowledge of the secrets of the kingdom of Heaven. He had revealed the mysteries of the kingdom to them.

Let's look at a passage from the Apostle Paul to the church at Corinth to help us understand this idea further:

> We are not like Moses, who would put a veil over his face to prevent the Israelites from seeing the end of what was passing away. But their minds were made dull, for to this day the same veil remains when the old covenant is read. It has not been removed, because only in Christ is it taken away. Even to this day when Moses is read, a veil covers their hearts. But whenever anyone turns to the Lord, the veil is taken away. Now the Lord is the Spirit, and where the Spirit of the Lord is, there is freedom. And we all, who with unveiled faces contemplate the Lord's glory, are being transformed into his image with ever increasing glory, which comes from the Lord, who is the Spirit (2 Corinthians 3:13-18).

Paul says that we are not like Moses, and he refers to a familiar Old Testament story. When Moses went into the tabernacle to meet with God, he would come out with his face shining radiantly. His face reflected the manifest presence, and glory, of God. So Moses gave the word of the Lord to the people, then he put a veil over his face because he did not want the people to see the glory fade from him. He couldn't stay in the presence of God; he had to go in and out of the presence.

Paul was making this amazing observation that we are not like Moses because now the Spirit of God lives within us. We do not need to go into the tabernacle to access God's presence; we have become the tabernacle and God's presence now dwells within us. We need to become aware of and sensitive to the presence of God within us. We need to learn how to walk in awareness of the presence of God, to walk in step with the Spirit.

Notice that Paul says the Israelites were blinded by a veil; this was the veil of religion. They had to come to faith in Christ to understand the meaning of the Old Testament. They needed revelation to make sense of what the Scriptures were saying about the Messiah. Freedom from the veil of religion is available in Christ and Christ alone. Paul says, "And we all, who with unveiled faces contemplate the Lord's glory, are being transformed into his image with ever increasing glory, which comes from the Lord, who is the Spirit" (2 Corinthians 3:18). There is freedom available to those of us in Christ. In Christ, the Spirit brings us revelation to take the things we have read and make them known to us. It is the Spirit that brings freedom.

Paul said to this same church, in his previous letter, that the Spirit of God has revealed the "mystery that has been hidden" (1 Corinthians 2:7). Paul wrote that the rulers didn't understand these things but "God has revealed them to us by his Spirit" (1 Corinthians 2:10). Paul goes on to talk about the revelatory work of the Spirit in these terms:

> The Spirit searches all things, even the deep things of God. For who knows a person's thoughts except the person's own spirit within? In the same way no one knows the thoughts of God except the Spirit of God.

We have not received the spirit of the world but the Spirit who is from God, that we may understand what God has freely given us. This is what we speak, not in words taught us by human wisdom but in words taught by the Spirit, explaining spiritual realities with Spirit-taught words. The person without the Spirit does not accept things that come from the Spirit of God but considers them foolishness, and cannot understand them because they are discerned only through the Spirit. The person with the Spirit makes judgments about all things, but such a person is not subject to merely human judgments, for, "Who has known the mind of the Lord so as to instruct him?" But we have the mind of Christ (1 Corinthians 2:10-15).

Many times our worldview or our theological biases blind us to biblical realities. We cannot break free from our blinders unless we humble ourselves before the Lord and position ourselves to receive revelation. Paul tells us that we cannot understand the things of God without revelation. It is not discerned through human wisdom or natural understanding.

An example may help here: many people in the Western world do not have a very robust spiritual worldview. So they dismiss demonization and deliverance ministries. I have even read of New Testament scholars, deeply committed to the truths of the Bible, dismissing the deliverance ministry of Jesus by saying those deliverances were just psychological problems, and that first-century people didn't understand such things. Now pause for a second: when we consider ourselves smarter than Jesus, something is seriously wrong with our worldview and the condition of our hearts! We need to humble ourselves before the Lord and realize we are missing something. We are in need of revelation. We are trying to make sense of spiritual realities with our human understanding, and we are blind though we do not realize it. Our Western worldview has blinded us to biblical realities. We need the Holy Spirit to take the things we read and make them known to us. We need revelation so that we can have eyes to see and ears to hear. But revelation can only be received by the humble of heart.

Many people know they are loved by God because they have read the verses in the Bible that tell them this. But even though they "know" they are loved by God, they are still living like unloved people. They are still insecure, defensive, and/or feel unloved at times. Why? Because they have knowledge without revelation. When you experience revelation about God's love, and the love of God is made known to you by the Holy Spirit, it shifts something deep inside of you. And you are moved from religious knowledge to revelation, from information to transformational experience.

When Jen and I went through our marriage crisis, I knew I was loved by God. I had read the passages. I had many of them memorized. I often preached on these things. I even had an encounter with Jesus in which I experienced His love. But I was not living like a deeply loved person in my interactions with Jen. So I meditated on God's love daily and put myself in a position to receive the revelation of the Holy Spirit about who I am in Christ. I listened to the Spirit's testimony about God's love in my heart (Romans 8:14-17). I did the work of renewing my mind and became determined to act as a deeply loved person with the help of the Holy Spirit. And as I did all this work, the Spirit did His job. He revealed to me the deep love of God, and it changed my life. I started acting like a deeply loved person and reflected Jesus' love to Jen more consistently in our marriage.

When we pride ourselves on what we know, and our knowledge doesn't lead us to become more loving, we are simply moving in religion. We have, too often, traded knowledge for revelation, but it is revelation that leads to transformation. You cannot be changed without the revelation and empowerment of the Holy Spirit. Paul said to this same church in Corinth: "Knowledge puffs up while love builds up. Those who think they know something do not yet know as they ought to know. But whoever loves God is known by God" (1 Corinthians 8:1-3). The true test of our spiritual maturity is not what we know but how we love. When the Spirit reveals things to us, rather than becoming proud, these revelations cause us to draw near to God and love God and people more.

Learned Behavior to Authentic Experience

If we are going to break free from religion and move into a deeper relationship with Christ, we must shift from learned behavior to authentic experience. Often when we are part of a group of people, we learn how we must behave if we are going to be accepted in that group. We learn to say the right phrases, do the right actions, and express the appropriate emotions. We learn to conform to certain cultural norms. We learn what phrases are not acceptable, what actions are inappropriate, and what emotions are illegal within that group. And we learn to conform so we can belong. This happens in families, it happens in people groups, and it happens in churches. The danger of this in your spiritual life is that you are substituting learned behaviors for authentic experience, and it may cause you to think you have arrived when you are actually missing out on the real.

We learn to read our Bible, pray, fast, go to church, and we do a bunch of the right things, but are we encountering Jesus in those things? We can do all the right things and still find ourselves missing Jesus' presence, His voice, His love, and His power. I don't want to substitute learned behaviors for authentic experience. I don't want to read the Bible, know the Bible, and teach the Bible without seeing the realities the Bible speaks of in my own life. To not see and live in those realities is empty religion. It is a counterfeit.

I have been involved in services where the Spirit of God was moving powerfully and filling hundreds of people at a time with His Spirit. Nearly everyone I laid hands on in those services was filled with the Spirit in a demonstrative way. For example, they cried or fell over under the powerful manifestation of the Spirit's presence. But sometimes in that setting I would go to pray for someone who was standing up because they wanted prayer to be filled with the Spirit, and as soon as I laid hands on the person, they started praying. "Yes, Lord. I need you, Lord. Help me, Lord." But these were just learned behaviors; they were religious phrases they had learned to say in church. Sadly, they were keeping the people from encountering God. Often I found the person was striving, not receiving. They were unintentionally making it too much about them and not enough about Jesus. On many occasions I would simply say to the person: "Shh. Don't pray. Just fix your eyes on Jesus and receive." And immediately they would start praying again: "Yes, Lord. Help me, Lord." Again, I would exhort the person: "Shh. Be quiet. Just receive." They couldn't. One day I was praying for a man, and I kept trying to coach him to receive, and finally I said, sternly, "Stop talking. Stop praying. Be quiet. Just receive." He did, and immediately the Spirit filled him in a powerful way. We have to stop doing our religious schtick and just lean into Jesus for the real. We have to stop doing all of the religious things we have learned to do that have become meaningless and simply hunger for God and seek Him for the authentic.

Contrast that with two people I prayed for recently. I was doing a Soul Care Conference in the Northeast, and after I completed a man's deliverance, he asked me to pray for him to be filled with the Holy Spirit. He was desperate. He told me he was a Baptist, had been reading *River Dwellers*, and longed to be filled with the Spirit. As he spoke, he burst into tears. I knew he was ready and had faith to receive. I had him stand up, and I laid hands on Him and simply said, "Come, Holy Spirit." And the Spirit came with power. He fell out and laid there for a long time under the loving, weighty presence of God.

I was in Australia and a pastor came to me, once again, desperate to be filled with the Holy Spirit. As I laid hands on him, he started weeping as the love of God was poured out in his heart, and the man grabbed my hand and pressed it to his chest so I wouldn't take it away, as the Spirit surged within him. Of course, it wasn't me doing anything, it was the Spirit filling him, encountering him, soaking him with God's presence and love. I found out later that when the man was filled with the Spirit he was also healed of an ailment that I didn't even know he had—Jesus threw that in as a bonus! Both of these men had come from religious backgrounds; they had grown up in church and learned all the right things to say and pray and do, but they had gotten to the place where they longed for something more, something real, something deeper with God. They had been passionately seeking, and God met them in a powerful, life-changing way.

Our job is to give up all our learned behaviors, phrases, and religious jargon, and just come after God with all our hearts. Our responsibility is to prepare our hearts to receive from the Lord by humbling ourselves and earnestly seeking Him, for Himself, not His benefits. Our part is to become enamored with and hungry for God's manifest presence, not manifestations. Our job is to cultivate longing in our souls for an authentic experience and encounter with God.

Sometimes what keeps people from authentic experience is their fear and resistance to things they have not experienced. I have prayed for people, for example, to be filled with the Spirit, but sometimes people have taken the time to tell me what they *didn't* want. They didn't want to speak in tongues, or they didn't want to experience holy laughter, or they didn't want to fall out when the Spirit came in power. They wanted God if He came on their terms. They were afraid—afraid of the manifestations, afraid of being embarrassed, and sometimes, if they were honest with themselves, afraid of the Holy Spirit. But fear of the Holy Spirit is demonic. Jesus isn't afraid of the Holy Spirit. Fear of the Holy Spirit is a tool of the enemy to keep you from freedom and fullness in Christ. It is the enemy's attempt to keep you from experiencing the deep wells of the Spirit and leave you stuck in the shallow waters of religion. The Holy Spirit is a good gift from the Father (Acts 1:4). We must deal with our fear, surrender it to God, and break down our resistance to the Holy Spirit. Jesus isn't resistant to the Holy Spirit. We seek God for Himself, not the manifestations. But we don't fear the manifestations if they come. When the Spirit comes in power there are sometimes manifestations, but they are merely manifestations of the Spirit's coming. Don't fake manifestations; that's just religion. Don't fear manifestations; that is religion too. Seek the Master, not the manifestation, and don't fake them, don't fear them, and don't be offended if you don't receive them.

Declaration to Integration

If we are going to move to an authentic spiritual life with Christ, we need to shift from declaration to integration. In many charismatic and Pentecostal traditions there is an emphasis on declaration. We declare the truth. We declare who we are in Christ. We declare all sorts of things over ourselves and our circumstances. Please hear me: I am not against declaration; I believe that has value. However, we need to go beyond this. It is a good beginning point, but it is not a good ending point. Declaration without integration leads to disintegration in our souls. We need to integrate these things into our lives. We have to take the truths we are declaring and learn how to live a life consistent with the truths we proclaim.

Many Christians "pray on the armor of God" every day. One day Martin Sanders and I were teaching an Alliance Theological Seminary class together and a woman from a very religious background said to us, "You two must pray on the armor of God all the time!" Martin said, "We never take it off." I laughed and said, "The armor of God isn't something that Paul intended for us to pray on; it is something Paul intended us to live out!" If you pray it on without living it out, it isn't going to help your life change. That's just superstition. Think about one specific piece of the armor as an example. *The belt of truth*: we don't have to pray on the belt of truth every day; we have to make sure we are living in the truth and living out the truth. I know I am deeply loved by God; that is true. But if I am living like an unloved person, and all the while "praying on" the belt of truth every day, is it doing me any good? That's just religion. I don't want to "pray on" the belt of truth; I want to *live out* the truth in my life. It doesn't do any good until I live like a deeply loved person—even when someone is criticizing me. It's easy to live like a deeply loved person when the people around me are loving me well, but what about when your enemies are stirred up against you? That's what Paul was concerned with: integration, not merely declaration.

We know God is good. We can declare all sorts of passages about the goodness of God over our life and circumstances every day, and that isn't a bad thing, I'm not against that. But if I am declaring that, and taking offense at God because He isn't doing what I want Him to do, my declaration isn't causing me to trust in the goodness of God. It is just a religious pattern that I have learned, and it doesn't lead to life change. I must process my offense and develop an active trust in God's goodness. I don't want to simply have all the right beliefs and declare them; I want my theology and doctrine to lead to holy living and active trust in a good Father. Otherwise, what good is it? James said, "You believe that there is one God. Good! Even the demons believe that—and shudder" (James 2:19). This is in the context where James tells us that faith without deeds is dead. If your faith doesn't lead you to freedom, fullness, and intimacy with God, it isn't doing you any good.

In many Evangelical environments there is an emphasis on declaring the truth as well, but it usually comes in the form of preaching good, solid, biblical doctrine. Listen: I am not against good, solid, biblical doctrine. In fact, I am whole-heartedly for it. However, too often we focus on declaring our version of the truth, which includes secondary doctrines, and we condemn those who disagree with us on these non-essential doctrinal points. Knowing the truth is important, but it doesn't make you mature. I have been called a heretic and a false teacher because of my beliefs, as I said earlier, but not one point of attack is a central Christian doctrine. I had a conversation once with a man who disagreed with me, and I said to him, "I would be happy to agree to disagree on the issue of whether or not Christians can have demons. We agree that Jesus is Lord. Jesus is the Savior. There is no other way to Heaven except through Christ, and likely we agree on every major doctrine out there. Let's just agree to disagree on this issue." He said, "I can't. You're a false teacher." I have given up trying to reason with unreasonable religious people. I haven't given up on loving my enemies, and blessing those who curse me, but I don't engage in these sorts of conversations anymore because you can never gain any relational ground. The unreasonable religious person has to have the last word. They have to be right and prove you are wrong, and that is religion.

Fenelon said, "We must not forget that God is both Truth and Love. We can only know the Truth in proportion to our love" (Fenelon, *Let Go,* Whitaker House, pp. 66, 67). The truth is that God is love. How can we say that we know the truth unless we are truly known for our love? If all our study of Scripture and all our engagement with spiritual disciplines doesn't make us more loving, something is seriously wrong with our spiritual life. The greatest mark of maturity is not our capacity to know, but our propensity to love. Are you more concerned with loving others well, even those you disagree with, or are you more concerned with being right and defending your interpretation of scriptural truth? When Jesus was asked what the most important thing is, He said to love God and love people. He didn't say the most important thing is to have every doctrinal point in order and argue with others who disagree with you. I ask you sincerely: is your life marked with the love of Jesus? Are you more loving this year than last? Do you love God and people more than you did? Do you love people who disagree with you? If not, then your life is likely marked with religion, and it is time to forsake the counterfeit and access the authentic.

Control to Surrender

The root of religion is fear, and fear often leads us to control. We control people with strictness, legalism, judgment, and shame. When someone grows up under this environment it often leads to rebellion. The Pharisees created environments of legalism, judgment, and shame to control people. Jesus said of the religious leaders of his day, "They tie up heavy, cumbersome loads and put them on other people's shoulders, but they themselves are not willing to lift a finger to move them" (Matthew 23:4). Yet contrast that with what Jesus said about Himself: "Come to me, all you who are weary and burdened, and I will give you rest" (Matthew 11:28). Jesus didn't come to burden us with more rules, stricter living, judgment, condemnation, and shame. Rather, Jesus came to give us rest from all the rules and control of religion. He didn't want us to substitute the bondage of sin for the bondage of religion. He wanted us to experience life, and life abundant (John 10:10). He came to set us free from sin and empower us to follow God without extraneous man-made rules.

Jesus said of the religious leaders, "You snakes! You brood of vipers! How will you escape being condemned to hell? Therefore I am sending you prophets and sages and teachers. Some of them you will kill and crucify; others you will flog in your synagogues and pursue from town to town" (Matthew 23:33, 34). The Pharisees were on a witch hunt. Anyone who disagreed with them or threatened their control and power became a liability to them—to the point that they were even willing to kill in the name of God. Sadly, they were blinded by their religion and missed the fact that they were killing the ones sent by God for their benefit, even killing the Messiah Himself, in the name of God.

I am always wary of people's angry responses in the name of God. I hear people go after others with whom they disagree and attack them with vehemence. They do it all in the name of God and see themselves as defenders of truth. But their level of anger and defensiveness points to a deeper reality. They are not full of truth and grace; they are often full of a narrow religious viewpoint and anger. Sometimes they claim it is "righteous anger." But I think angry people who are unwilling to examine their motives use that as an excuse all the time. If it is truly righteous anger then it cannot involve self at all. Righteous anger is always for another's benefit, not because our control gets threatened or someone hurts us or disagrees with us. Righteous anger cannot be associated with personal offense. When Jesus is angry in the temple, He isn't angry because of anything anyone did to Him; there is no personal offense against Him. He is angry because the religious leaders are oppressing people in the name of God. When Jesus is nailed to the cross unjustly, on the other hand, He displays no anger at all. Rather, He prays, "Father, forgive them, for they do not know what they are doing" (Luke 23:34). When we are claiming our anger is righteous, but our motive is selfish, we are lying to ourselves. That is religious spin. Also notice that Jesus isn't on a witch hunt for truth violators or false teachers; the Pharisees are on a witch hunt for Jesus. God, help us to be on the side of Jesus, not on the side of the Pharisees.

In Second Corinthians there were false apostles trying to deceive the people, so Paul defended his apostleship (note that he did not defend himself) because he didn't want the church to walk away from God. In that context Paul writes, "For if someone comes to you and preaches a Jesus other than the Jesus we preached, or if you receive a different spirit from the Spirit you received, or a different gospel from the one you accepted, you put up with it easily enough" (2 Corinthians 11:4). Notice what he points out as false teaching: a different Jesus, a different spirit (other than the Holy Spirit), a different gospel. When you see one of the New Testament writers equipping the church to combat false teaching, it is not over secondary matters of preferential opinions. False teaching in the New Testament is always a compromise of the primary issues. One of the members of the Trinity is falsely presented; or the gospel has become about works, not about faith; or the teacher is engaged in morally reprehensible behavior.

There has been a great deal of debate recently over the subject of women in ministry. I want to use this topic as an example, and I am happy to graciously disagree with those who hold a different position, and I would ask you to do the same. I am an egalitarian; I believe women should be able to teach, preach, and lead in the church. I'm also a firm believer in the authority of Scripture. I believe there are strong biblical reasons to be an egalitarian or I would not take that position. For those who believe women should never speak, there are two passages that are always referred to: 1 Corinthians 14:34-35 and 1 Timothy 2:11-12. 1 Corinthians 14:34, 35 says, "Women should remain silent in the churches. They are not allowed to speak, but must be in submission as the law says. If they want to inquire about something, they should ask their own husbands at home; for it is disgraceful for a woman to speak in the church." But in 1 Corinthians 11:5, Paul gave women instructions for praying and prophesying in church. This is the same passage where he tells them to cover their heads. Now, notice two things: first, most of us do not follow the head covering passage (with a few exceptions) because we consider it cultural; second, Paul is allowing women to speak in the church—praying and prophesying is speaking in the church. So clearly he didn't mean that they can't speak in the church as a universal rule.

In 1 Timothy 2:11, 12, Paul writes, "A woman should learn in quietness and full submission. I do not permit a woman to teach or to assume authority over a man; she must be quiet." Yet in the book of Acts Paul partners with Priscilla and Aquila. This couple is mentioned six times in the New Testament: in Acts 18:2, 3; Acts 18:18, 19; Acts 18:26; Romans 16:3-5; 1 Corinthians 16:19; and 2 Timothy 4:19. They are always mentioned together as a couple, and in four of the six mentions, Priscilla is listed first. This is not insignificant. The Gospels tell us that Peter and John often partner together—but it is always Peter and John, never John and Peter. That is because Peter is clearly the leader. Priscilla, who Paul calls his coworker (Romans 16:19), has become the leader of this team. The only two occasions where she is not listed first are Acts 18:2, 3, where we are introduced to them as a couple for the first time; and in 1 Corinthians 16:19, where Aquila comes first. Isn't it possible that there were certain New Testament church-specific situations where Paul did not allow the women to teach and lead, but that was not his practice in all situations, since he partners with Priscilla and Aquila? Paul is not an inconsistent person, so when I see inconsistencies between what Paul writes and how Paul practices ministry in the book of Acts, I can only conclude that there are very good historical, contextual reasons for Paul writing what he writes in these two passages that are often quoted and disputed. I am not giving a thorough defense of my reasons for being egalitarian here; I am merely illustrating that there is a good biblical reason to believe this is a cultural issue, not a universal one.

Now please hear me: I would be happy to partner with people in ministry who are gracious complementarians. I would not break fellowship with people over this issue. Nor would I call another a false teacher simply because we disagree. I would be pleased to graciously disagree and focus on the essential things we have in common: our belief about Jesus, the Father, the Spirit, the Gospel, and our mission to take the message of Jesus to the world. However, there are people who cannot discern secondary issues, and they make every disagreement a "gospel" issue. I have heard people argue that those who are egalitarians are "compromising the gospel." That simply is not true. This is not a gospel issue. This is not a false teaching issue. In the New Testament corrections of false teachers are never used for anything other than a false teaching about the Trinity or the Gospel (that is, that we can be saved through faith in Christ alone; through His life, death, and resurrection) or someone who is proclaiming the gospel for spurious motives while not following Jesus. When we are threatened, we often seek to control. Many times people in charge feel threatened when they start to lose power, and they seek to control. This happened with the Pharisees and Jesus. Often people feel threatened when they feel like their long-held beliefs are being challenged and their understanding of those beliefs are being changed. It makes us feel uneasy and unstable, and we want to stabilize our situation by regaining control. It makes us feel insecure, like the foundations are being torn away, and we fight with a vehemence that belies there is something more at stake than simply the issue being discussed. We are fighting for control so often because we are afraid. This is part of religion, and if we are going to move from religion to the authentic, we need to give up control and move to authentic surrender.

We talked about surrender earlier; let me add just one thing here. Let's finish quoting the passage I began with from Jesus: "Come to me, all you who are weary and burdened, and I will give you rest. Take my yoke upon you and learn for me, for I am gentle and humble in heart, and you will find rest for your souls. For my yoke is easy and my burden is light" (Matthew 11:28-30). In the face of the heavy burdens of religion, Jesus offers us an alternative, lighter route. He offers us His yoke. He is calling us into submission, surrender. There is freedom in surrender to Jesus. There is no freedom in religion. There is no freedom in trying harder, in doing more in an attempt to feel accepted, in seeking to gain control over our lives and the lives of those around us. There is freedom in surrender. Often in this agricultural society farmers would pair two oxen together in one yoke so the two beasts could share the load and pull together more effectively. Jesus is calling us to pull toward righteousness under His power, not under rules, and not under guilt, shame, condemnation, or control. He is calling us to bow our stiff neck and join Him. Let Him lead wherever He will take us; we are to simply say yes and follow no matter what. I can tell you that it has not always been easy for me to surrender to God, but I have always found freedom when I did. There is no freedom without surrender. And when we still feel bondage, unsettledness, a lack of peace, and anger bubbling within us, it is so often because we have not truly surrendered. Jesus loves you, and He is truly good. You can trust Him. Take up His yoke, bow your stiff neck, and surrender. Only then can you know freedom and peace.

Temporal to Eternal

If we are going to make the shift to the authentic Christian experience, we are going to have to shift our focus from the temporal to the eternal. When we fix our attention on the temporal, we look for our satisfaction from the temporal, and temporal things become idols. Then when things in the temporal do not give us what we long for, we are often disappointed and even take offense at God. If we don't walk away in rebellion, we stagnate in resignation, and our relationship with God is filled with more religiosity than authenticity.

As we noted, Jesus said that the most important commandment is to love God (Matthew 22:37). Jesus confronted the church at Ephesus because the believers there had lost their first love (Revelation 2:4). Jesus wants us to love God first because God is the most important person. He isn't being selfish; this is the highest good for us because of who He is. This is why

God calls us to put Him first, as our number one priority and primary love. We must order our priorities and our loves in their proper order or life doesn't work the way it was designed to work. Only God can truly satisfy; if we put something before God, we will be empty. It is for our good that God calls us to love Him first. Jesus doesn't forbid us to love others; as a matter of fact, in the same conversation in Matthew 22, He said that the second most important command is to love our neighbors as ourselves. Jesus doesn't forbid us to love things on earth—sunsets, houses, nature, possessions, or pets—He simply calls us to order our loves properly so our lives will flourish accordingly. When Jesus ceases to be our first love and our primary obsession, we end up trying to get our sense of satisfaction and life from the temporal rather than the eternal. These temporal things cannot satisfy; they are not lasting. They were designed to point us to God, not take the place of God. We are trying to draw life from something that cannot give life. God is the source of life, and only God can give us life and life abundant (John 10:10). God and His eternal kingdom must take priority in our lives.

When Jesus sent out the Twelve, He warned them of persecutions to come, but He assured them that they didn't need to be afraid. However, He wasn't saying they didn't need to be afraid because He would protect them, that nothing bad would happen to them, and that everything would work out. He said, "Do not be afraid of those who kill the body but cannot kill the soul. Rather, be afraid of the One who can destroy both soul and body in hell. Are not two sparrows sold for a penny? Yet not one of them will fall to the ground outside your Father's care. And even the very hairs of your head are all numbered. So don't be afraid; you are worth more than many sparrows" (Matthew 10:28-31). He wasn't guaranteeing them a harm-free life. He said we do not need to fear those who have the power to kill us.

Jesus said "do not be afraid" to these disciples even though He knew they were going to suffer and die for their faith. He wasn't saying we don't need to be afraid because He will make everything work out to our advantage in the temporal realm. It won't. He wasn't saying we don't need to be afraid because we won't have hardships in this life. We will. He wasn't saying we don't need to be afraid because we won't be hurt, persecuted, or even killed. We might be. The apostles certainly were. He was simply saying we don't need to be afraid because He holds eternity in His hands. We don't need to be afraid because our Father lives in Heaven. We don't need to be afraid because Heaven is eternal, and earth is temporal, so whatever happens here is fleeting, but our rewards for following Him through hardship will be never-ending. Your good Father lives in Heaven. He sees. He cares. He has you. He holds eternity in His hands. Whatever may come, whatever may happen in this temporal world, you do not need to be afraid because you are a child of your eternal heavenly Father. Live with an eternal perspective and you will live with a fearless focus. Live with an eternal perspective and you will rightly order your loves and priorities.

This is why we must shift our focus from the temporal to the eternal. When our focus is on the temporal, we pray temporal prayers. We are consumed with the material world. We pray for material blessings—jobs, promotions, raises, convenience, comfort. Our prayers become focused on our temporal well-being—happy marriages, good children who grow up healthy and get good jobs and live in good neighborhoods and have good relationships. Again, these things aren't bad—unless they take priority over our first love, and our eternal citizenship. Unless we are looking to them for our comfort and satisfaction. When they win space in our hearts over Jesus, they become an idol, and they rob us of abundant life. If we are focused on the temporal and are praying accordingly, when things don't work out we get upset, hurt, and angry with God; we become anxious, fearful, sad, and worried. We deaden our hearts to God; we take offense because God isn't meeting our needs. But really, the problem is that our priorities and the things we love are not in proper order. We have overvalued the temporal and undervalued the eternal. We have made life too much about us and not enough about Jesus, and we have lost our way. Like the church of Laodecia in the book of Revelation, we have become lukewarm. Our temporal focus has robbed our hearts of our first love. And like them, we do not realize that we have become "wretched, pitiful, poor, blind, and naked" (Revelation 3:17). And to us, as well as them, Jesus says, "Whoever has ear, let them hear what the Spirit says to the churches" (Revelation 3:22).

I have had to battle for an eternal focus and for Jesus to be my first love and primary obsession. Sadly, most often what has interfered with my eternal focus and first love is my self-ishness. I have made life too much about me far too often. I have discovered the only time I am miserable in marriage is when I make life too much about me. I begin to ask: what about me? What about my needs, my wants, my feelings, my desires, my hopes, my plans, and my opinions? This is also true of my relationship with God. When my focus is on me, and life isn't going the way I want, it has led me to be hurt and offended by God. When my focus is on Jesus, and His eternal

Kingdom and His honor, I am willing to endure hardship for His sake and can even take pleasure in the fellowship of His suffering. The apostles rejoiced when they were persecuted because of this eternal mindset. There have been times when the thing that robbed me of my eternal focus and first love was ministering for Jesus. I became focused on results. Sometimes the results I focused on were promises from God that I was praying for, but they were delayed in coming. And again, because of self-focus and misplaced passions, I was hurt and offended by God.

As I said earlier, I finally got to the place in my life where I made a covenant with God that I would never take offense again. He has proven His goodness; He has proven His faithfulness. He has delivered me from countless situations. He has redeemed marriage pain to produce Soul Care, which has been used for life change for hundreds of thousands of people around the world. He redeemed ministry pain and attacks to produce spiritual authority that led to far more of His power and supernatural activity in my ministry. I have seen how He can redeem pain to shape my life and advance His kingdom, so I made a choice that I would never take offense at God again. That choice changed my life. I decided it was childish to continue to take offense. I was behaving like a child throwing a tantrum and demanding God prove His goodness to me over and over. He proved His goodness on the cross, and He has proved His goodness through His redeeming work in my life. It was time to simply choose to trust Him no matter what. Most of my offenses came down to making it too much about me, and too much about the here and now, and not enough about Jesus and the eternal.

I would ask you these simple questions:

- Is Jesus truly your first love and primary obsession?

- Is your focus more eternal or temporal?

When Jesus is not our first love, and eternity not deeply settled as our primary focus, we will inevitably allow some religiosity to replace authenticity. We need to repent, die to self, and get our focus back on Jesus and eternity.

Passive Faith to Active Faith

If we are going to shift from religion to authentic experience with God, we need to develop a deep, active trust in God. We have to shift from a passive faith to an active faith. Passive faith often includes belief in solid doctrine without integrating those beliefs into our everyday life. Passive faith often consists of religious expressions void of deep experience. For example, I talk to people who go through suffering, and they say, "Praise the Lord. God is good all the time." That is true, but you can tell when they haven't processed the grief, they haven't gotten in touch with the pain, they haven't done the work to come out the other side of the tunnel and into the light. We have to go through the tunnel of processing pain in order to get to the light of deep trust.

We looked at the Apostle Paul and his response to suffering earlier in the chapter: he rejoiced in his weakness so that Christ's power would be perfected. But before he rejoiced, he processed. He asked God to remove the suffering. He felt the pain; he sought relief. He leaned into the Lord, and when the Lord explained why it was necessary, he trusted God and surrendered. Notice that Paul had a personal revelation from the Lord that led to deep transformation. This kind of processing is utterly essential for a true, active, deep trust in God.

Paul was steeped in an eternal focus, which I believe makes it easier to process suffering. When we view suffering through the lens of eternity it makes more sense, it has more meaning, it becomes more endurable. We can rejoice in the fellowship of suffering with Christ, Jesus can redeem our suffering to form Christ in us, and Jesus can reward us for our suffering in eternity; nothing is wasted. Paul writes the letter to the Philippians from prison, and he says that some people are preaching Christ so they can cause Paul more trouble than he is in already (Philippians 1:15-17). Paul's remarkable response to this is, "But what does it matter? The important thing is that in every way, whether from false motives or true, Christ is preached. And because of this I rejoice" (Philippians 1:18). Paul was well acquainted with suffering, but his eternal focus allowed him to put it in perspective. It allowed him to stop making life too much about him and to focus on Jesus and the advancement of the gospel. He put Jesus' eternal cause above his temporal comfort, and ultimately he knew he would be rewarded, in Heaven, for suffering.

Again, notice that Paul acknowledges the truth about his situation. It is painful. People are committing evil. But his true citizenship is in Heaven, so he can endure suffering with Christ so Christ's kingdom can advance. Paul goes on to say, "For to me, to live is Christ and to die is gain" (Philippians 1:21). Paul knows that, in light of eternity, it is better for him to die and be with Jesus. But if he is going to live here on earth, he is going to live for Christ, and he isn't expecting that to be an easy life. He signed up to follow the God of the cross, and hardship is part of his assignment.

I love reading authors who have suffered well for Christ because they have an unusual depth to their souls. They face their suffering in alignment with Christ. They don't take offense at God, or if they do, they work through that offense and surrender to God. They, along with Paul, learn to embrace suffering in a redemptive manner. Paul said to the church at Philippi, "I want to know Christ—yes, to know the power of his resurrection and participation in his sufferings, becoming like him in his death, and so, somehow, attaining to the resurrection from the dead" (Philippians 3:10, 11). Paul, and all New Testament writers, understood that for us to experience Jesus' resurrection power (and deep relational connection to Jesus), we must first experience the cross of Christ. Suffering well is essential to deep intimacy. Death to self is critical to abundant life. We must embrace the cross if we are going to experience Jesus' power in and through us. This theological understanding of the cross, along with Paul's eternal perspective, gave him a totally different faith-lens on suffering. Suffering is part of following, and Paul expected it and learned to rejoice in it. Not rejoice that he suffered, but rejoice that God redeems the suffering, rejoice that God will reward the suffering, rejoice that he could share in Christ's suffering, and rejoice that well-processed suffering would lead him to a deeper intimate experience with the risen Christ. Paul could also rejoice that the cause of Christ was often advanced through the suffering of believers. These weren't just spiritual phrases that Paul bantered about in times of hardship; these were deep experiential truths that Paul knew and spoke of from well-processed pain and active trust in the God of the cross.

If we lay religious phrases over unprocessed painful experiences, we won't develop deep faith. Our faith remains shallow, and this hinders our intimacy with God. Learning to truly trust God in pain is essential to developing active faith.

Passive faith leads to resignation at best. We resign because there is nothing else we can do except rebel, and we don't want to rebel. But we don't really trust God. Of course, we often say we do because that is what we are expected to say, but they are shallow words and lack true restful surrender. There is an incongruity between our words and our life. Resignation often leads to joyless Christian living and a bit of a defeatist attitude.

Our lives are more harmonious when we have true trust. A life of active faith is characterized by peace, joy, love, and the fruit of the Spirit. A life of active faith is marked by God's presence, power, and abundant life. We don't minimize pain with easy solutions and quickly quoted religious phrases. There is an otherworldly stillness about a person who has processed pain, been marked by the presence of God, and developed deep faith. There is a weightiness to their words when they speak because they are words of wisdom that come from healed pain, eternal rootedness, and lessons born in suffering. They don't feel a need to speak in rooms filled with people to be noticed; they don't fill silence with religious verbiage. They release timely words that are measured by the Spirit and carry Jesus' healing balm. There is an inner peace and rest that marks a person who has learned to embrace the cross, process their pain, and actively trust God. They are not easily offended by God or people because they carry the security of heavenly citizenship in their hearts, not merely their heads. They are marked by grace because they have experienced the work of the cross. They are known by their love because the pain has sanded down much of their self-life. When they speak of God, they don't speak as one who knows the right answers about God, they speak as one who has been with God. God help us to suffer well and develop authentic faith.

Passive faith is often connected to fear. We can either act on fear or act on faith, but we cannot act on both. We can choose to act on faith when we feel afraid, but we must choose which one we will act on. Too often, when our faith is passive, we say the right things, we can quote the right verses, but fear is still the driving force of our choices. When we are ruled by fear, that's not authentic faith. Rather, our faith is weak and passive.

When our faith is marked by fear, we avoid some conversations because we are afraid of the pain or discomfort they will cause. We are afraid of displeasing people or falling out of favor. When our faith is marked by fear, we may engage in other conversations in an aggressive, angry way because we are afraid when people don't agree with us. We are afraid of rejection, or we are afraid of being minimized, embarrassed, or insignificant. When our faith is marked by fear, we avoid certain risks because we are afraid we will fail, look dumb, or be shamed. At other times when our faith is marked by fear, we take reckless risks because we are marked by a bravado rooted in shame. We must make something of ourselves to prove to ourselves and others that we are somebody, so we take foolish risks, not by the leading of the Spirit, but by the shame in our soul. When our faith is marked by fear we are afraid of being found out, not being "enough," not being loved, not doing enough, not getting it right, not being accepted, not belonging. When our faith is marked by fear we wrestle with perfectionism and control. When we are marked by fear we feel threatened when people disagree with us, and we passionately and aggressively protect what we believe because of our insecurities.

We have to deeply internalize God's love because perfect love casts out fear (1 John 4:19). We must learn to rely on

God's love, not merely acknowledge that we are loved by God (1 John 4:16). This enables us to get free from fear and develop deep faith. We trust someone deeply when we know we are loved by them. Paul said, "The Spirit you received does not make you slaves, so that you live in fear again; rather, the Spirit you received brought about your adoption to sonship" (Romans 8:15). The adoptive love of the Father is the antidote to fear-filled, passive faith.

I learned how to rely on God's love when I went through my marriage crisis. I had to get to the place where I knew I was loved by God, and God's love was enough for me, even if Jen left me. I learned how to rely on God's love even more when I went through the spiritual attacks for years. I learned to internalize the love of God and to begin to act like a deeply loved person in my daily interactions. Again, I haven't perfected it. I am still learning, but I am so much better than I used to be. But it didn't happen passively. Every day I did the work of relying on God's love, asking myself how a deeply loved person would act in this situation, and living life like I was deeply loved. Obedience forged true faith. Biblically speaking, the opposite of faith is not doubt; the opposite of faith is unbelief that leads to disobedience. When I say that I know I am deeply loved by God, but I live like an unloved person, that is not authentic faith. When I "know" that God is good, but I am taking offense over situations, I am not trusting the goodness of God. That is a passive faith that is underdeveloped and full of doubt. Doubt is not a sin, but it is underdeveloped faith we must address so our lives can be consistent with what we say we believe. If we never chose to address our weak faith, God will still love us, but we will live well beneath our life's potential.

I had a conversation with someone recently who was trying to help their adult child make better decisions. I said to them that they only have four tools to help another person change. You can have a conversation where you speak the truth in love—full of truth and full of love, like Jesus (John 1:14-18). If the person hears you, understands, but refuses the advice, then you need to let it go. If you continue to have the conversation, you are seeking to control the situation. That's not true trust in God. At that point you only have three tools left: love, wait, and pray. Love them as they are, wait for them to be open for another round of conversation, and pray for them and for that opening in their heart. This is where we have to throw ourselves on God in trust—this is active faith. We are not just saying that we trust God and yet continuing to attempt to control things. We are actually learning to trust God in real time. The person I was speaking with cried and said this kind of trust is so much harder to live. It is hard, but this is what real faith looks like, and it is incredibly rewarding. This is why we have to make the shift from passive faith to active faith.

Sin Management to True Holiness

If we are going to develop a deep, intimate relationship with Jesus, we must shift from sin management, or behavior modification, to true holiness. Too often in religious contexts our definition of holiness is askew. Holiness becomes about a list of do's and don'ts. If we are "holy," we think, we will do these things and not do certain other things. But this was the "holiness" of the Pharisees, not the holiness Jesus spoke of. The holiness Jesus spoke of included behavior but went down deep to the motivations of the heart. The holiness of the Pharisees was driven by human effort motivated by shame. The holiness of Jesus is fueled by our acceptance by God and empowerment by the Holy Spirit.

Often in religious circles we measure maturity by what people believe and how people behave. Those things are important. But Jesus went beyond that. Jesus measured maturity by the heart. In most religious circles someone can be considered mature if they have good doctrine, know their Bible, pray, fast, go to church, aren't found to be in an adulterous affair or financial shenanigans, and don't have some dark secret life. But this could be said of many of the Pharisees, and does anyone want to say those who killed Jesus were holy? They lacked the most fundamental thing: they didn't love well. They didn't love God, they didn't love God's Son, and they didn't love people. How can we be holy if we are not most of all characterized by love? This is the thing that Jesus said mattered most. When the measure of our maturity is characterized more by the rules of the Pharisees then the love of Christ, something is seriously wrong with our faith.

One of the teachers of the law came to Jesus to test Him and asked which is the greatest commandment. Jesus' response was simple: "'Love the Lord your God with all your heart and with all your soul and with all your mind.' This is the first and greatest commandment. And the second is like it: 'Love your neighbor as yourself.' All the Law and Prophets hang on these two commandments" (Matthew 22:37-40). Listen: it is not complicated. If you're not growing in love, you are not growing in an authentic, intimate relationship with Jesus. Are you more loving this year than you were last year? Do you love God more? Do you love people more? When people are with you, do they feel Jesus' love through you? When people are with you, are they inspired to love Jesus and others more? If not, then likely your faith has become more religious than authentic. You have settled for a counterfeit. I don't say this to shame or embarrass or harm; I say this because it is most likely true, and it is not yet too late to change. Repent. Admit this to God and others. Call out to the Lord for a heart change, and don't stop crying out to God until you have what you ask for—because He has promised He will do this for those who call upon Jesus.

Sadly, in too many churches we have acted as if Jesus' first commandment is to be right all the time, and to defend the truth with anger and vehemence and to guard our rights. In our zeal for our Christian faith, we have misrepresented Jesus to those around us and to each other. And at times we have been more like Pharisees than like Jesus. I reiterate: truth is important. We should be people of the Word. I have read my Bible cover to cover nearly one hundred times, and I have read the New Testament, and portions of the Old Testament, hundreds of times. I love the Bible because it leads me to Jesus. But I don't want to use the Bible to attack those who love Jesus but disagree with me. I would rather we agree on the big issues about the Trinity and salvation and agree to disagree with gracious generosity on nearly all other matters. I would be happy to dispassionately discuss these other matters in love, and come back again and again to our first love for Jesus. But when our first love is more closely associated with being right than it is being with Jesus, something is off in our souls. When we cannot agree to graciously disagree with those who love Jesus, what is underneath that? That is not about truth, that is about our brokenness. That is not about being right, it is about the need to be right. If you are attending a church that is like this, seek to make a difference or find a new church. If you are living a life that is like this, take a new path. If you are a pastor and you are like this, please wrestle with what is in your soul.

Years ago I was teaching a Soul Care Conference and there was a woman attending who was visibly standoffish to me. I didn't know why, but I didn't take it personally. Soul Care is a three-day conference. Near the end of the second day, I walked past her and smiled, and she stopped me. She said, "I wish I could get a do-over for this conference." I laughed and asked why. She told me she was best friends with someone who had blogged against me and attacked me publicly. This blogging friend had negatively influenced her opinion of me. So she came with her arms folded across her chest both literally and figuratively; she was skeptical, critical, and resistant. But then she surprised me when she said, "But I have watched you for two days and I realize that you have what I have always wanted. You love God with a deep, passionate love, and you love people—even people who don't love you back. That's what I have always wanted. That's why I wish I could get a do-over, so I could listen without all the resistance." That dear woman came to several more conferences, and I have always been blessed by her presence; she changed the path she was on. I will never forget that conversation. I want to be a man who loves God and loves people like Jesus. Sadly, I have not always represented Jesus well. I too at times have held to my beliefs without grace and love. At other tinmes, I too have been more interested in being right than in being in a right relationship. But I am growing, and I am consciously focused on seeking to represent Jesus well in all human interactions.

I think this is what holiness is all about: representing Jesus well to all we encounter. It is about representing Jesus well in our families. I need to represent Jesus well to Jen, to my adult children, and to my grandchildren. I want to represent Jesus well to my neighbors who do not know Him. When we moved into our house, there were some upset neighbors. Most people viewed one man as an angry man who was to be avoided. But there was another side to this man. He was the one who snowplowed the street we all share in common. When Jen and I moved in, we didn't realize it was a private road and that we needed to help with clearing the snow from the street. So, every storm, this disliked man was out there by himself, and I was often away traveling. Once I realized it, I helped, but all I had was a shovel at the time, yet no one else on our little street helped. He was also fiercely protective of his yard. He didn't want people to hit his grass with their tires, so he put boards with nails in them on the edge of his property. The nails were pointing up so that anyone who drove into his yard would pop their tires. Some of the neighbors complained to me about it and, to them, it simply confirmed their conviction that he was an unreasonable, angry man. But when spring came, Jen and I bought our snowplowing neighbor a gift certificate to a local restaurant and wrote him a thank you note of appreciation for all the effort he had put in to keep our road clear over the winter. We wanted to love him and bless him, and he has become a friend. My goal is to represent Jesus well to my neighbors with love, grace, and generosity. He has been a great neighbor to us.

I want to represent Jesus well to my friends and my enemies. Maybe especially to my enemies. Jesus said even pagans love their friends; what credit is that to a Christ-follower? But loving our enemies is the true mark of the Father's touch on our hearts. That is a clear sign of God's divine love changing us. So I bless those who curse me, forgive those who sin against me, and seek to love my enemies because this is Jesus' way. I want to love people who don't believe as I do, don't act as I do, don't live as I do. This is Jesus' way.

During the season of ministry attacks that I faced, there was one man who attacked me more vigorously than any other. One day I did a wedding for a mutual friend, and this man who had attacked me and done me a great deal of harm came to the wedding. I didn't try to avoid him. I had already forgiven him even though he never apologized for his actions. So when I saw him, I went over to greet him, gave him a hug, and talked to him cordially for a minute before I moved on. I didn't think much of it, but that week I received an email from a young man who had come to faith in our church. The young man had left our church because of this other man's influence. The young man wrote to me and said, "For years while I attended your church, I listened to you speak about forgiving those who sin against you, but I didn't really believe you. I thought you were just saying it because you were the pastor and that is what you were supposed to say. Then I watched you interact with that man who had done you so much harm. I know what he said about you, and I know what he did to hurt you. And I realized you meant what you were preaching because you lived it. I want you to know we will be coming back to the church because you live what you preach."

In all that you do, in everyone you interact with, represent Jesus well, and that always begins with love. This has become my holiness standard and goal. Paul said that "love is the fulfillment of the law" (Romans 13:10). I just want to represent Jesus well. Jesus, full of truth and grace, didn't come to condemn anyone but to save everyone who would follow Him.

Am I representing Jesus well to everyone in my life? Are you? When you blow it, make sure you apologize for your words or actions. Though Jesus never sinned, I do believe apologies represent Jesus well, because Jesus was humble, and only humble people apologize.

Self-Reliance to Spirit-Empowered Living

If we are going to live an authentically deep spiritual life in Christ, we need to shift from self-reliance to Spirit-empowered living. We need to learn how to live in the power of the Holy Spirit. I grew up going to church, but I didn't learn how to live by the power of the Spirit. When I surrendered my life to Christ in college, I had a significant encounter with the love of Jesus that changed me. I immediately broke free from some sin patterns, other sinful behaviors held less of a grip on me, and others I continued to struggle with. I had to learn to yield myself to the Holy Spirit issue by issue and moment by moment—and I am still learning. I had to discover how to work out my salvation with fear and trembling and learn to listen to the Holy Spirit and surrender to Him. I had to learn how to give Jesus access and appropriate His victories.

He taught me to be honest, and to walk in the light with Him and others, and I found more freedom. But I had to yield myself to His direction when He called me to walk in the light. He taught me to depend on His love when Jen didn't love me, but I had to decide to renew my mind and start to live like a deeply loved person even while, at times, I still felt insecure and unloved. This process of learning to surrender to the Spirit, hear His voice, obey His promptings, and draw from the strength of His presence within us is vital to living an authentic Christian life. Otherwise we are living a life as a Christian under our own empowerment, and that is not the life in Christ presented in the New Testament.

I want to talk about three key aspects of learning to live life in the Spirit. There are many more things we could speak of, but these three are critically important for our study.

First, **we have to learn how to hear the Holy Spirit speak.** In John 10:27, Jesus said, "My sheep hear my voice" (ESV). I know some people say that God only speaks through the Bible. But that isn't what the Bible says. In Acts 2:17, 18 Peter says, "'In the last days, God says, I will pour out my Spirit on all people. Your sons and daughters will prophesy, your young men will see visions, your old men will dream dreams. Even on my servants, both men and women, I will pour out my Spirit in those days, and they will prophesy.'" The promise of God is that He will pour out His Spirit, and all of His children will hear His voice: young and old, male and female. This will characterize the end times which, in the New Testament, is the period of time from when Jesus rose until Jesus returns. We are in the end times, biblically speaking, and therefore we should hear God's voice.

When you read through the book of Acts, you see God speaking to people. Let's do an extremely quick survey. In Acts 5, God lets Peter know that Ananias and Sapphira are lying. God speaks to Philip, the deacon, in Acts 8, and leads him to speak to a eunuch who decides to follow Jesus and is baptized. In Acts 9 Jesus reveals himself to Saul, and He tells a man named Ananias, through a vision, to lay hands on Saul. In Acts 10 Peter receives a vision from the Lord that instructs him that Gentiles are to be included in the church, and Cornelius and his family are converted. In Acts 13 Paul and

Barnabas are set apart for missions through a word from the Lord in a season of fasting and prayer. In Acts 14 Paul "sees" that a man has faith to be healed. In Acts 16 Paul receives a vision of a man from Macedonia and knows the Lord is calling him to preach the gospel there. This isn't an exhaustive list of prophetic occurrences in the book of Acts; it is simply to indicate the overwhelming testimony in this great book that the Holy Spirit was speaking to people—just like Peter said He would in his Acts 2 address.

In both *River Dwellers* and *The Soul Care Leader* I write about how to hear God's voice. But I want to give you a very practical tool here to help you get started. One of the best ways to train yourself to hear God's voice is to meditate on Scripture. Nearly every day I read a passage from the Gospels and try to pay attention to the Spirit's stirrings within me as I read. Sometimes as we read Scripture carefully, slowly, with a heart that is prepared and open to the Lord, He will highlight something to us. A phrase, or a word, or a particular action will stir something inside of you. Linger there. Ask the Holy Spirit for insight. Ask the Spirit to speak to you about the passage. Ask for revelation, illumination, and supernatural insight. Ask the Spirit to apply the passage directly to you. What is God saying to you personally here? We looked at Paul's writings to the Corinthians earlier and took note of how Paul said we cannot understand the mind of God without the revelation of the Spirit. We need to put ourselves in a place to receive the revelation and illumination of the Spirit by linger-ing with a passage of Scripture and seeking to stay sensitive to what the Spirit is showing us. This is one of the ways we can train our ears to hear what the Spirit is saying.

Then spend time quieting your heart and listening for the voice of God. All prophetic words need to be tested by Scripture. If you receive a word that disagrees with the Bible, it is not from the Lord. Once we learn how the Spirit speaks to us, we can learn to be more sensitive to His direct revelation as we quiet our hearts before the Lord and to His leadings throughout our day. Every day I sit before the Lord in qui-et and listen for the Spirit to speak directly to me. I remove the things that hinder me from being sensitive to God's pres-ence—like making sure my confessions are current, process-ing my negative emotions, and praying through my to-do list. Then I listen for the Lord's direct revelation.

How can we have a personal relationship with God if we don't know how to hear His voice? Every other personal re-lationship I have is a dialogical friendship. We can't develop intimacy with someone who doesn't communicate directly to us. I believe we can hear God through Scripture, but Scripture also tells me that the Holy Spirit speaks directly to me, and hearing God's voice has greatly enhanced my intimacy and journey toward holiness. We just looked at how, in the book of Acts, God was speaking directly to His people. The Spirit reveals God to us and words from God to us; I have experi-enced this. He has poured out the love of God in my heart (Romans 5) in various encounters. He has testified that I am a deeply loved child of God (Romans 8). He has led me to root issues I needed to address and surrender to God which resulted in breakthroughs in my life. Hearing God's voice has been critically important in my journey to holiness and intimacy. We need the Holy Spirit's voice to live a supernaturally empowered life, and we need supernatural empowerment to represent Jesus well.

Second, if we are going to shift to a life empowered by the Spirit, **we not only need to listen to the Spirit, we need to obey Him.** We need to say yes to God no matter what He asks us to do. The Holy Spirit led me to confess to my wife that I was struggling with lust in the middle of our marriage crisis. It didn't seem like a good idea to me. It would not have been a choice I would have made. But when I surrendered to God and obeyed the Spirit, it led me to a breakthrough, and it was one of the keys to us moving forward in our relationship. The Spirit called me to stop defending myself in our conflict resolution conversations. It was not a natural path; again, I wouldn't have thought of this on my own. It was the direction of the Holy Spirit, but when I obeyed, it changed the dynamic of our conversations, and it was critically important for me to start acting like a deeply loved person. It allowed me to see new things about myself that eventually led to breakthroughs. I started making significant progress on solidifying my identity in Christ and integrating God's love into my daily life.

The Holy Spirit knows how to make you holy. He knows what you need to say yes to and what you need to say no to. He knows the roots to your presenting problems. Too many of us are focused on the fruit and not the roots. We cut off the top of the weed hoping it will not grow back, but we don't address the root—the issue of the heart—and we continue to wrestle with the same problems year after year. The Holy Spirit taught me to go after the heart and soul issue, to get to the root issue, and this has led to many victories in my life. Religion so often focuses on behavior management, sin management, and image management but doesn't lead us to victory. The Holy Spirit focuses on the heart and soul and leads us to Spirit-empowered breakthroughs. We have to hear His voice and trust Him enough to say yes—no matter what.

> The Holy Spirit focuses on the heart and soul and leads us to Spirit-empowered breakthroughs.

Third, if we are going to live a Spirit-empowered life, **we must cultivate a sense of His presence and learn to walk in step with the Spirit.** Paul wrote: "Therefore, there is now no condemnation for those who are in Christ Jesus, because through Christ Jesus the law of the Spirit who gives life has set you free from the law of sin and death. For what the law was powerless to do because it was weakened by the sinful nature, God did by sending his own Son in the likeness of sinful humanity to be a sin offering. And so he condemned sin in human flesh, in order that the righteous requirement of the law might be fully met in us, who do not live according to the sinful nature but according to the Spirit" (Romans 8:1-4). We could not overcome our sinful nature and obey the law of God on our own. So Christ paved the way for us to be forgiven and acceptable as righteous before God by becoming a sin offering for us. But He didn't leave us there—forgiven yet helpless to change. He gave us the Holy Spirit so that we can live a victorious life. But we have to learn how to live "according to the Spirit." The Christian life is meant to be a supernatural life lived by the presence and power of the Holy Spirit. He helps us appropriate the victories of Jesus in our lives. Therefore, we must develop a sensitivity to the Spirit's presence and voice; we must learn how to depend on the Spirit's help and power.

We looked at 2 Corinthians 3 earlier. Let's look back at vv. 17, 18: "Now the Lord is the Spirit, and where the Spirit of the Lord is, there is freedom. And we all, who with unveiled faces contemplate the Lord's glory, are being transformed into his image with ever increasing glory, which comes from the Lord, who is the Spirit." The Spirit of God is the key to our holy living. We cannot do it on our own; it is impossible. We need the Holy Spirit. Paul said that we "contemplate the Lord's glory." The Spirit of God is deposited within us when we put our faith in Christ. Now we must learn to become sensitive to His presence and His voice. It's like marriage. I had to become sensitive to my wife's feelings, needs, and wants. I had to learn how to "read" her. I was lousy at it in the beginning; that was one of the reasons we had conflict. I would offend her and not pick up on it. I remember after we were making our way out of the marriage conflict, one year for her birthday I wrote out for her a bunch of "coupons" she could cash when she wanted to do so. They were all things I had learned that mattered to her, things that made her feel noticed and loved. She read through the coupons, cried, and said, "You understand me." Some people call that "emotional intelligence"; it is learning how to be self-aware and sensitive to the feelings of others around us. We learn how to treat others with dignity and respect, sensitivity and honor. It is the same with the Holy Spirit. We must develop a sensitivity to His presence and voice, and we must learn how to honor Him and how to stop "grieving" the Spirit (Ephesians 4:30).

In the beginning of my walk with God I would often speak defensive words, angry words, and words of power that came out of my insecurity and brokenness. I didn't know why I was doing it, and I wasn't sensitive to how it was hurting others and grieving the Holy Spirit. I would feel "off" afterward; almost like I had too many cups of coffee. It took me a while to realize this was the conviction of the Holy Spirit. I was brand new to walking in step with the Holy Spirit; nobody had taught me how to do this. It took me a little time to realize that my words had grieved the Spirit and offended someone He loved, and I needed to apologize. When I followed through, the peace of Christ would return, and harmony would return to my relationships. Eventually the Holy Spirit led me not only to be sensitive to His presence and His voice, and to repent, but to deal with the root issues causing these hurtful words.

Too many people today are Bible people without being Spirit people. I do not believe you can be a Bible person, but not a Spirit person, without being religious. Are you a Spirit person? Are you living by the Spirit, listening to His voice, walking in step with Him, living empowered by Him? Paul said to the church at Galatia, "You foolish Galatians! Who has bewitched you? Before your very eyes Jesus Christ was clearly portrayed as crucified. I would like to learn just one thing from you: Did you receive the Spirit by observing the law, or by believing what you heard? Are you so foolish? After beginning with the Spirit, are you now trying to finish by human effort?" (Galatians 3:1-3). We can't be saved by our

> Too many people today are Bible people without being Spirit people. I do not believe you can be a Bible person, but not a Spirit person, without being religious.

own effort; we cannot be sanctified by human effort. We have to be born of the Spirit to be accepted into God's family, and we must be empowered by the Spirit to live a holy life. It took faith to receive salvation and the deposit of the Spirit; it takes faith to learn how to cultivate His presence, hear His voice, and walk in His strength. We cannot live the Christian life by being good Bible people only. We must be Word and Spirit people. How sensitive to the Holy Spirit's presence and voice are you? How marked by His presence and empowered by the Spirit is your life?

Self-Life to the Christ-Life

If we are going to live an authentic Christian life, we must shift from the self-life to the Christ-life. In Galatians 2:20, Paul writes, "I have been crucified with Christ and I no longer live, but Christ lives in me. The life I now live in the body, I live by faith in the Son of God, who loved me and gave himself for me." I think the most important thing I have learned that I am responsible for in my journey toward holiness is the significance of death to self, which is part of humility. Jesus told us, "Whoever wants to be my disciple must deny themselves and take up their cross daily and follow me. For whoever wants to save their life will lose it, but whoever loses their life for me will save it" (Luke 9:23, 24). There is no victory without death to self. There is no peace without surrender. There is no sanctification without denying ourselves. There is no resurrection

> There is no victory without death to self. There is no peace without surrender. There is no sanctification without denying ourselves.

power without the cross. Death is the key to life; the cross is the gateway to the resurrection.

As I said earlier, the only time I am miserable in my life is when I am making life too much about me. Too much about my wants, my needs, my desires, my opinions, and not enough about Jesus and others. When my heart is focused on Jesus and doing what He wants, I am not miserable, I am free and full. If my heart is focused on pleasing others, I eventually burn out and feel resentful. That is because I am really still focused on me; I want other people's approval so I can feel good about myself. If my heart is focused on getting what I want, I am pretty miserable.

The more I die to self, the more Christ lives in me. The more I take up my cross, the more I experience Jesus' resurrection life. The more I yield myself to the Spirit and say no to my selfish desires, the more I find freedom and joy in my soul. I never feel joy when I am focused on what I want but do not have. I feel anxious because I don't have that thing, or I feel angry because I want it and can't obtain it. Or I feel jealous because someone else has it and "I should have it." Or I feel sad because I am being kept from what I perceive I need. When I am focused on myself, I don't feel love, joy, and peace. Only when I die to self, and say yes to the Lord, are love, joy, and peace restored.

This has become so clear to me that now when I lose my love, joy, and peace, and I am feeling a little misery, I get a block of time alone with God to figure out where I have lost my way. Where am I making life too much about me? What do I need to die to? What do I need to surrender to the Spirit? I seek the Spirit for insights to the root of the issue, and I die to self, so Christ can live in me once again—and love, joy, and peace are restored.

Our self-life is that part of us that is self-focused, self-centered, self-protective, self-defending, self-reliant, self-sufficient, and sometimes just plain selfish. Our self-life is our greatest impediment to our freedom. Ironically, here in the West, we often encourage self-fulfillment: do what you want, don't let anyone tell you what to do or who you are, you are who you say you are, and you can do whatever you want to do. These things become the keys to "self-fulfillment." But, in truth, they aren't. Often they simply lead us into more bondage and less freedom. More anger and misery, less peace and joy. More selfishness and hatred, less sacrifice and love. Death to self is the key to life abundant. Go God's way, not your way. It is one of the contrary ways of the kingdom.

> Our self-life is our greatest impediment to our freedom.

I wish I could tell you that I have died to self and I no longer live, just like Paul wrote. But that isn't true about me. I still battle with my self-life. I wish I could say I no longer get hurt when people criticize me, but sadly, sometimes I still do. It takes me less time to get through the offense. I don't spend much time, anymore, in my mind in imaginary conversations or desiring to defend myself so I can set the record straight, but I do still feel the hurt, angst, pain, and anger, and I have to process through it many times. I can often work through it and get back to feeling and acting like a deeply loved child of God within minutes; it used to take me days. But the old self-life is still there, and it still rears its ugly head far more than

I wish it did. I am on to his game, though. I know his tricks. He is trying to pull me into making life more about me, deceiving me into believing that this is the key to abundant life, to self-fulfillment, to peace and joy. But it isn't. Our self-life is like the Sirens in Ulysses' *Odyssey*. They cry out with their beautiful song and lead the sailors to pursue their compelling voice. They sing with an irresistible urgency, an unmatchable beauty, and the sailors follow that song right into the rocks and to their deaths. So it is with my self-life: it sings the Siren song of self and calls me to crash on the rocks of misery. For many years I have been learning to die to self, to say no to those urgent songs, and to say yes to Jesus. I have been learning that the way of the cross is the way of the resurrection, that you must die to live. I have been discovering that I have been sold a bill of goods; I have been deceived. And I have decided I do not want to play by the rules of self any longer.

I wish I had discovered these truths years ago. I guess I knew these things to be true. I read about them in the Bible and in some ancient writers, and to some degree believed them to be true. But I didn't believe them enough to live them, and I didn't understand them enough to see that I was making life way too much about me and that this was causing me grave misery. That's the nature of religion: we know things that we don't live, but we don't realize we aren't living them because we know about them. Jesus told us that if we want to save our life, we will have to lose it. Fortunately, I believed Jesus enough to keep coming back to

> That's the nature of religion: we know things that we don't live, but we don't realize we aren't living them because we know about them.

this truth. I kept reading writers who spoke about death to self as the key to the Christ-life. I kept meditating on passages that spoke of this reality, passages like Luke 9:23, 24 and Galatians 2:20. Fortunately, issue by issue, the Spirit kept leading me to the root; He kept calling me to die to self. The more I died, the more I lived. The more I lived, the more I longed to die to self. Finally, I discovered that the root of most of my misery was my self-life, and I determined to let it rule over me no longer. This is why I have read Fenelon's *Let Go* more than fifty times: he has discipled me into death to self, and I have discovered the life of Christ is on the other side of a cross.

Where are you struggling in your self-life? Where are you making life too much about you? Where is Jesus calling you to take up your cross and follow Him? Where has your self-life led you astray to the point of being miserable? Are you willing to die to self, surrender to Jesus, and discover His resurrection power? This is authentic Christian living. But religion always makes life too much about us, and there is no life there.

COVID revealed how deeply attached to our rights and opinions we are. There was so much division in the church, and many, if not most, divisions are caused by self-life. James said, "What causes fights and quarrels among you? Don't they come from your desires that battle within you? You desire but do not have, so you kill. You covet but you cannot get what you want, so you quarrel and fight" (James 4:1, 2). During COVID we fought over masks or no masks, vaccines or no vaccines, political persuasions right and left. We revealed that we were more American than we were Christian. We were more Republican or Democrat than we were eternal citizens. We were more white, black, Asian, and Latino than we were citizens of Heaven. We were more attached to our rights

If we want to live a supernatural, authentic Christian life that is transformative and transformational to those around us, it will only come because we pick up our cross and die to self. This is the path of Jesus.

and opinions than we were to Jesus and the cross. And so we fought, we divided, and Satan laughed at our impotent religious self-centeredness and our opinionated squabbles.

If we want victory, it will not come because we are strongly attached to our opinions, or because we are committed to fighting for our rights. The only right we have, as Christ-followers, is the right to pick up our cross and follow Jesus. If we want to live a supernatural, authentic Christian life that is transformative and transformational to those around us, it will only come because we pick up our cross and die to self. This is the path of Jesus. This is the path of resurrection power. This is the path that marks us with God's presence. There is no other way. Other than that, we will be left with a lot of our self-life intact, with religiosity and without authenticity. We will be left with a counterfeit and robbed of the true supernatural life Jesus has planned for us. That's not the life I want. How about you?

Conclusion

FINISHING WELL

I was listening to the Bible on Audible, and a story from the Old Testament grabbed my attention. I listened to the end of the story, and then I went and lingered in the story for about a week. I did this because I sensed there was more there that God had to say to me. I felt that old familiar stirring of the Spirit, and I knew the Lord wanted to meet me in this narrative. The story is about a king of Judah named Asa.

Let me set the context. If you have read the Old Testament, you know that the Israelites constantly pushed God to the edges of their lives. God called them to put Him at the center of their individual lives, their family, and their community, but they kept pushing God to the edge. He was still there, but they weren't centered on God. They worshiped other deities; they engaged in the immoral practices of the surrounding nations. They didn't take holiness seriously. It is a repetitive story. Enter Asa. "Asa did what was good and right in the eyes of the Lord his God. He removed the foreign altars and the high places, smashed the sacred stones, and cut down the Asherah poles. He commanded Judah to seek the Lord, the God of their ancestors, and to obey his laws and commands" (2 Chronicles 14:2-4). Asa took God seriously; he put God at the center of his life and the life of the people. He tore down the foreign altars and high places. He led a reform and moved the people toward renewal.

God hates hypocrisy. He wants us to be honest and authentic. He doesn't want us to pretend to be something we are not. He doesn't want us to keep Him at the edges of our life while we keep up a good front, put on a good show, and try to present ourselves as good Christians. When we push God to the edges of our life but continue to go through the motions of doing the things Christians are supposed to do, acting "Christian" on the outside, but far from God on the inside, that's hypocrisy. When we are more interested in looking good than being good, that's hypocrisy. When we are more closely associated with the attitudes and mindset of the Pharisees than we are with the heart of Jesus, that's hypocrisy. Before I surrendered my life to Christ at 19, I lived in this way. I read my Bible, went to church, acted like a Christian with my Christian friends, and yet I lived differently when I was with my non-church friends. I wasn't living a wildly sinful or immoral life. God was still in my life, but not at the center of my life. I had enough fear of God that I had moral restraint,

> God hates hypocrisy. He wants us to be honest and authentic. He doesn't want us to pretend to be something we are not.

but God was not the central character in my existence. I didn't make my decisions based on what God wanted. For the most part, I made my decisions based on what I wanted.

That was often how the Israelites lived—until Asa started his reforms.

As Asa takes these serious steps toward reform, a crisis arises. It isn't uncommon. We make a decision to put God at the center of our lives, and we undergo testing. Some of it is the enemy of our souls. He sees we are putting God at the center, and he wants to do everything he can to dissuade us. Some of it is God's doing. God never tempts (see James 1), but He does test. James makes it clear that the testing of our faith is to develop perseverance, and perseverance is necessary to make us mature and complete. If we are going to be like Jesus, we must go through testing. And we must pass the tests. Jesus never gives anyone a test so they will fail that test; Jesus gives us tests so we will master kingdom living.

Back to Asa's time: the Cushite army comes to attack Judah. It is a much larger army than Judah's and poses a serious threat to Judah's survival. "Then Asa called to the Lord his God and said, 'Lord, there is no one like you to help the powerless against the mighty. Help us, Lord our God, for we rely on you, and in your name we have come against this vast army'" (2 Chronicles 14:11). Asa doesn't rely on his own wherewithal or military might, and he doesn't rely on other nations. He turns in true, active trust to the Lord, and the Lord delivers. Asa and the people of Judah pass the test—and the renewal takes even deeper effect.

When the Lord called me to preach revival until it comes, the enemy stirred up people to attack me. The Lord assured me they were not my enemy; these people were merely duped by the enemy. But I had to pass the test. I blessed those who cursed me. And I stayed the course. When the attacks started, I went to the Lord, and asked, "Why?" Not "Why me, poor me," but "Why is this happening, why are people responding like this?" And I heard the Lord say, "I'm answering your prayers." I joked with God, "I don't know what I have been praying, but if you tell me, I promise I'll stop." I had been praying for revival. I had studied the history of revival. I had noticed that often in times of revival the flame of revival was passed on from person to person and place to place, through impartation— the laying on of hands would quicken the spread of the fire of the Spirit. Peter and John lay hands on the Samaritans, and they are filled with the Spirit (Acts 8). Ananias lays hands on Paul and he is filled with the Spirit (Acts 9). Paul lays hands on the Ephesians and they are filled with the Spirit (Acts 19). This happens throughout history as well. So I had been praying: "Lord, give me the ability to impart your Spirit like that—if my character and intimacy can sustain it." I had also studied revival and noticed that far too often people started seeing a great move of God, but the move was cut short because the leaders blew up their lives. They didn't have the character and intimacy necessary to handle the power and success they experienced. So I prayed for the character and intimacy necessary to sustain that anointing, and the Lord set about to answer my prayer through testing.

He told me: "This is what it takes."

Amidst these attacks, I was afflicted with self-doubt. I kept asking, "Am I doing the right thing?" People were attacking, yet I was just trying to follow Jesus' lead in my life to the best of my ability. Did I get it right? Whenever I asked the Lord, "Am I doing the right thing?" I would hear, "Keep your hand to the plow and do not look back." More attacks would come, and I would question again: "Am I doing the right thing?" The Lord would say again, "Keep your hand to the plow and do not look back." About six months into this, one day a woman came up to me at church. She was a visitor, and she said: "Pastor, I know you don't know me well. But I had a vision today when you were up there speaking. You were standing behind an old hand plow. You were plowing an old field and it was full of rocks and roots and thorns and thistles. You were sweaty and grimy and weary, but you would not quit."

Keep your hand to the plow and do not look back.

The attacks continued. Periodically, I kept slipping into self-doubt, and I kept hearing the Lord say the same thing to me: *put your hand to the plow and do not look back.* About another year went by, and I was teaching at a Soul Care Conference at the church I pastored. A man came up to me after a session. He said: "I know you don't know me. But while you were teaching, I had a vision of you. You were standing behind an old hand plow. You were plowing an old field. It was full of rocks and roots and thorns and thistles. You were sweaty, and weary, and worn out. But you would not quit. And God is so pleased with you."

Keep your hand to the plow and do not look back.

After that long season of attacks, which went on for about five years, I went into a season of discouragement and a dark night of the soul. But I kept my hand on the plow. I kept pursuing God. To the best of my ability, I kept doing what the Lord wanted me to do. And after a long season of testing, I experienced a fresh encounter with the Spirit that resulted in a tremendous increase in God's power. God answered my prayer for impartation, but not without the test.

AUTHENTIC

If we are going to live authentic Christian lives of depth and intimacy, we must go through times of testing without taking offense at God and without quitting. We must allow the times of testing to make life less about us and more about Jesus. We must persevere and allow the testing of our faith to make us mature and complete, just as James exhorted us.

Once again, back to Asa: God sends the king a prophet to give him a word of encouragement after the victory over the Cushites. "The Spirit of the Lord came on Azariah son of Obed. He went out to meet Asa and said to him, 'Listen to me, Asa and all Judah and Benjamin. The Lord is with you when you are with him. If you seek him, he will be found by you, but if you forsake him, he will forsake you'" (2 Chronicles 15:1, 2). Asa received this prophetic word of encouragement and proceeded to double down on his reforms. "When Asa heard these words and the prophecy of Azariah son of Obed the prophet, he took courage. He removed the detestable idols from the whole land of Judah and Benjamin and from the towns he had captured in the hills of Ephraim. He repaired the altar of the Lord that was in front of the portico of the Lord's temple . . . They entered into a covenant to seek the Lord, the God of their ancestors, with all their heart and soul. . . They sought the Lord eagerly, and he was found by them" (2 Chronicles 15:8-15).

When we decide to put God at the center, there are tests designed to refine us, but there are also signs of favor. We must hold on to these signs of favor and persevere through the tests. Asa received a prophetic word. The people went all in with Asa. They received rest on every side. The Lord's presence marked their lives and their land. Life will be hard whether we follow God or whether we don't. Life is hard because we live in a fall-

Life will be hard whether we follow God or whether we don't. Life is hard because we live in a fallen, broken, sin-marred planet. But life is much harder without God at the center of our lives.

en, broken, sin-marred planet. But life is much harder without God at the center of our lives. Life is much harder when we are not sweetly accompanied by God's empowering, comforting presence. When we put God at the center, life is hard still, but we are marked by God's presence with us, strengthening us, encouraging us, tenderly loving us through the hardships. That is the story of the Israelites. That is my story, too. I've asked you before, and I will ask you again: is Jesus your first love and primary obsession? Is Jesus at the very center of your life? This is the most important thing. If not, humble yourself and go hard after God to make this right.

Again, back to Asa. If only the story ended there. Sadly, it does not. And I guess this is why it grabbed my attention that day recently when I was listening to it. For thirty-five glorious years Asa reigned with God's favor raining down on him. But in 2 Chronicles 16 another enemy attacks Judah, and this time Asa fails the test. He does not turn to the Lord; he does not rely upon the Lord. Instead, he turns to another nation for deliverance. He does not display an authentic, active trust in the Lord his God. He still is religious, he still is going to temple, reading his Bible, and praying. But his faith has become passive, not active. He comes up with man-made solutions and doesn't rely on the Lord. He still wins the battle against his enemy, but at what cost?

"At that time Hanani the seer came to Asa king of Judah and said to him: 'Because you relied on the king of Aram and not on the Lord your God, the army of the king of Aram has escaped from your hand. Were not the Cushites and Libyans a mighty army with great numbers of chariots and horsemen? Yet when you relied on the Lord, he delivered them into your hand. For the eyes of the Lord range throughout the earth to strengthen those whose hearts are fully committed to him. You have done a foolish thing, and from now on you will be at war'" (2 Chronicles 16:7-9). God is looking for people who are centering their lives on Him and actively trusting Him. They find what God wants, and they do it at whatever personal cost.

Asa has a chance to repent, to humble himself before the Lord. One of the beautiful things about the heart of God is that it is never too late to repent. As long as you have breath, you can repent. God is irresistibly drawn to the contrite of heart. God has more grace than you have sin. The only thing that keeps us from receiving it is pride.

> God is looking for people who are centering their lives on Him and actively trusting Him. They find what God wants, and they do it at whatever personal cost.

I am reminded of the story of king Ahab; his wife was Jezebel. He was about as bad a human as one can be. But at the end of his life, he repented. Look at God's remarkable response, "Then the word of the Lord came to Elijah the Tishbite: 'Have you noticed how Ahab has humbled himself before me? Because he has humbled himself, I will not bring this disaster in his day'" (1 Kings 21:28, 29). God relented from bringing judgment on a man who had lived in rebellion and wickedness his entire life because he humbled himself at the very end. It is hard to overestimate the magnanimity of God. God's grace is greater than all our sin. This is the God that I know; this is the God I love.

Asa had a chance, even in this hour, to humble himself. But he refused. Sometimes the Lord's correction comes when we are reading Scripture; sometimes it comes through a book like this one. Sometimes the Lord will correct us through a prophetic word or the word of a friend or even the word of an enemy. Sometimes the Lord will correct us through the conviction of the Spirit. But whenever the Lord corrects us, however it comes, there is only one proper response: we must humble ourselves before Him. We cannot resist. We cannot harden our hearts. We cannot argue and defend and justify our wrongful attitudes and actions. We cannot do those things and receive the Lord's loving presence, forgiveness, and favor. We cannot remain hard-hearted and draw near to God. If we remain on this hard-hearted course we will quench the Spirit. Sadly, that is what Asa does.

"Asa was angry with the seer because of this; he was so enraged that he put him in prison. At the same time Asa brutally oppressed some of the people" (2 Chronicles 16:10). How tragic. This is why the story captured my attention. How can someone start so strong and finish so poorly? How can someone walk with God for thirty-five beautiful years and rebel so horribly at the end? I hate this story. But I am glad it is in the Bible because it serves as a solemn warning to all of us. God sends Asa a sickness, in his feet, because he is walking the wrong path. It is another opportunity for him to change course. But still Asa refuses to repent; Asa refuses to humble himself and rely on the Lord. Thirty-five years of favor are tragically and unnecessarily followed by five years of rebellion, warfare, and sickness.

Here is the main point: humility is the one indispensable human quality necessary to welcome the presence and favor of God into our lives. Humility is the essential ingredient for intimacy with God. God is always willing to dole out His favor. God is always willing to mark us with His presence. The only thing that keeps us from being lavished with God's favor and God's presence is our pride. Like Asa, religious people begin an unnoticed slide from authentic humility to religious pride, and they grieve the Spirit and miss out on the favor of God.

> Humility is the one indispensable human quality necessary to welcome the presence and favor of God into our lives.

I've noticed that often hardship brings us to the ragged edge of desperation where we humble ourselves and cry out to the Lord. That's what happens to Asa in the beginning of the story. It is often during crisis that we turn to God with humility. That was true of me during the breakup, the marriage crisis, and the ministry attacks. But I've also noticed that sometimes when life gets a little easier we become more comfortable, fall into religious routines, and lose the ragged edge of desperation that leads to authentic humility. We slide into pride unwittingly. Our heart loses its soft, penetrable accessibility to God. It becomes a heart of clay, or even stone. A little more self-centered, a little more self-reliant, a little more concerned with our rights and our opinions, and a little less concerned with God's kingdom, and we sadly drift into a pharisaical religiosity. A little more concerned with comfort and less concerned with the cross, and we lose the resurrection power of the authentic Christ-life. We slowly drift into spiritual apathy, even self-righteousness or hardness. We become more judgmental and less gracious, more proud and less humble, more angry and less kind. When I begin to sense this shift in my heart I know I need to go after this heart condition with all that I have within me. I usually begin with a fast. I almost always set up a time to get alone with God for an entire day, and I humble myself before the Lord. I call out to the Lord for a soft heart, a contrite heart, a fresh touch from His Spirit. I beseech Him for an awakening of my first love for Christ. And I don't leave my fast or time alone with God until I have dealt with the obstructions to my authentic humility and experienced God afresh again.

A Proverb writer observed a field one day and wrote to us so that we might have ears to hear and eyes to see. He wrote: "I went past the field of a sluggard, past the vineyard of someone who has no sense; thorns had come up everywhere, the ground was covered with weeds, and the stone wall was in ruins. I applied my heart to what I observed and learned a lesson from what I saw: A little sleep, a little slumber, a little folding of the hands to rest—and poverty will come on you like a thief and scarcity like an armed man" (Proverbs 24:30-34). I suspect that Proverb writer is far more concerned with souls than fields, and he is pointing us to a deeper reality. He is saying that when we do not tend to the condition of our heart, when we do not take responsibility to keep our heart contrite and humble before the Lord, when we do not do the work to break up the fallow places of pride, one day we will wake to a life overcome by entropy. The unguarded heart will be robbed of God's flourishing presence. So much of our spiritual thriving is dependent on cultivating a humble heart before the Lord.

What is the condition of your heart today? Is your heart broken, contrite, and humble before the Lord? Are you experiencing authentic intimacy and depth with Jesus? Do you love Jesus more this year than you did two years ago? Do you love people more? When people are with you, do they love Jesus and others more because you are marked by love? This is the kind of life I want to live. I don't want to go through the motions. I don't want to simply read my Bible, pray, fast, go to church, tithe, serve, and live a decently moral life. I want to love God with all my heart, and I want to represent Him well in all my interactions. I'll never be perfect at it, so I want to be humble and admit when I am wrong. I want to abide in Christ and see His presence mark my life for His glory.

I want the authentic. How about you?

ABOUT THE AUTHOR

Dr. Rob Reimer's passion is to see the Kingdom of God advance through spiritual renewal. Rob began Renewal International to assist pastors, leaders, and churches globally to equip the people of God to live in freedom in Christ, and to walk in the fullness and power of the Holy Spirit.

Passionate about Jesus, personally transparent, and saturated in the Word, his books—including *Soul Care, River Dwellers, Spiritual Authority, Deep Faith, Pathways to the King, The Soul Care Leader, Calm in the Storm* and *The Tenderness of Jesus*—incorporate lessons God taught him over the years through life, marriage, and ministry. During conferences, Rob not only teaches these lessons but provides activities for participants to begin working them into their lives. These transformative experiences challenge people to walk in the light with God and others and help people to practice hearing from God and accessing His power for ministry. Without Jesus, we have nothing to offer!

In addition to his work with Renewal International, Dr. Reimer has served as Professor of Pastoral Theology at Alliance University in New York City, and as the founding and lead pastor of a church in New England.

To access eCourse, live, or video teaching on *Soul Care*, or to explore more of Rob's work, view his itinerary, or to invite him to speak, please visit www.renewalinternational.org.

ALSO BY DR. ROB REIMER

River Dwellers
Living in the Fullness of the Spirit

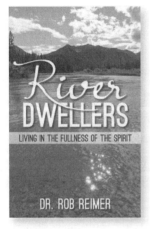

Did you ever wish there was more to your Christian life? Too often the Christian life is reduced to going to church, attending meetings, serving God, and doing devotions. But Jesus promised us abundant life—a deep, intimate, satisfying connection with the living God. How do we access the abundant life that Jesus promised? The key is the presence and life of the Holy Spirit within us.

Jesus said that the Spirit of God flows within us like a river – He is the River of Life. But we need to dwell in the river in order to access the Spirit's fullness.

In *River Dwellers,* Dr. Rob Reimer offers a deep look at life in the Spirit and provides practical strategies for dwelling in the River of Life. We will explore the fullness of the Spirit, tuning into the promptings of the Spirit, walking in step with the Spirit, and developing sensitivity to the presence of God in our lives. This resource will guide you toward becoming a full-time River Dweller, even in the midst of life's most difficult seasons when the river seems to run low.

Together let's become River Dwellers, living where the fullness of God flows so that we can carry living water to a world dying of thirst!

Pathways to the King
Living a Life of Spiritual Renewal and Power

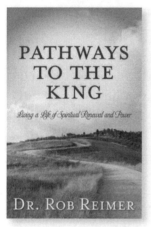

We need revival. The church in America desperately needs revival. There are pockets of it happening right now, but we need another Great Awakening. About forty years ago, the church was impacted by the church growth movement. The goal of the movement was to get the church focused on the Great Commission—taking the Good News about Jesus to the entire world. The church was off mission, and the movement was a necessary course correction. But it didn't work. Many people came to Christ as a result of this outreach emphasis, and I am grateful for that. More churches are now focused on evangelism, helping people come to know Jesus, than they were before the movement. But we have fewer people attending church now (percentage-wise) than ever before in the history of the United States. We need revival.

This book is about how we can usher in revival and also about the price that we must pay to experience it. I believe we have a part to play in seeing the next great spiritual awakening. God wants us to be carriers of His kingdom. He wants us to experience the reality and fullness of His kingdom, and He wants us to expand the kingdom to others—just like Jesus did. In order to do that, I believe we must follow eight Kingdom Pathways of Spiritual Renewal: Personalizing our Identity in Christ, Pursuing God, Purifying Ourselves, Praising, Praying

Kingdom Prayers, Claiming Promises, Passing the Tests, and Persisting. These eight pathways are discussed in great detail, are securely rooted in biblical truths, and are illustrated by compelling examples from Scripture and from my life, the lives of believers in my community, and in the lives of great Christians throughout history.

Available at www.DrRobReimer.com

Deep Faith
Developing Faith that Releases the Power of God

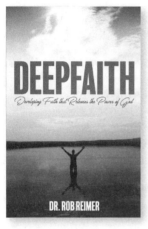

Jesus said, "Very truly I tell you, all who have faith in me will do the works that I have been doing, and they will do even greater things than these" (John 14:12). The extraordinary promise of Jesus is that we can do Kingdom works that He did—cast out demons, heal the sick, save the lost and set the captives free.

Jesus wants to advance His Kingdom through us. But this promise comes with a condition: the level of our Kingdom activity is dependent upon our faith.

There are promises in Heaven that God wants to release, but they cannot be released without faith. There are miracles that God wants to do that cannot be done without faith. There are answers to prayer that God wants to unleash that cannot be unleashed without faith. There are works of the Kingdom that God wants to accomplish that cannot be accomplished unless the people of God develop deeper faith. But there is hope for all of us, because faith can be developed.

Faith opens doors and creates opportunities for accessing God's power against all odds. Faith is a difference maker, a future shaper, a bondage breaker, a Kingdom mover. In this book, Dr. Rob Reimer challenges readers to develop deep faith that can release the works of the Kingdom. Faith is not static; it is dynamic. We can and must take an intentional path toward developing our faith if we want to see the works of the Kingdom in greater measure.

Spiritual Authority
Partnering with God to Release the Kingdom

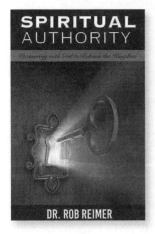

Jesus gave His disciples authority to preach the good news of the kingdom of God and to cast out demons, heal the sick, save the lost and set the captives free. Everywhere Jesus went, the kingdom came with power. There was no proclamation of the gospel without a demonstration of power. It was the authentic demonstration of Jesus' power through His followers that ignited the greatest spiritual movements in the first century. Today, we are becoming more like the spiritual climate in the first century than like 1950 America. In a pluralistic, syncretistic society where all deities are considered equal, only the unequal display of Jesus' power will convince people of the supremacy of Christ. The key to demonstrating the power of the King is Authority and authority is not just positional; it is developmental. Spiritual authority is rooted in identity, expanded in intimacy and activated by faith. This book takes an in-depth look at how we can grow in identity, intimacy, and faith so that we can develop our authority and release the kingdom.

Also available in Spanish (Autoridad Espirituald).

Calm in the Storm

How God Can Redeem a Crisis to Advance His Kingdom

There is nothing like a crisis to reveal the cracks in the walls of our soul. But God promises to redeem all things that come into our lives to make us more like Jesus. We are experiencing a unique crisis in our day and age, COVID-19. It has created fear, death, and will leave economic disaster in its wake. In this book, I don't just want to talk about how we can survive this crisis, or how we can access the peace of God in tumultuous times. I want to talk about how God can redeem a crisis in our personal lives to take us deeper into maturity and intimacy with Christ. And how this particular crisis could potentially lead to revival if the church processes it well. We stand on the precipice of an unprecedented opportunity to be purified and mobilized on mission to advance the Kingdom of God in our generation.

The Tenderness of Jesus

An Invitation to Experience the Savior

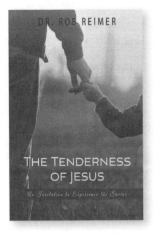

The world is a broken place marred by evil, and evil's influence impacts us all. It is often difficult for people to grasp what God is like in a world such as ours. Jesus shows us the heart of God in a world of heartache. He is the most beautiful, compelling, tender person who has lived.

Jesus is the radiance of God's glory. He shines forth what God is like; He is a beacon of light that cuts through the darkness of evil and radiates the goodness of God. He is the exact representation of God the Father. If you want to know what God is like, look to Jesus. Don't look through the lens of evil or the lenses of either the church or religion. Look to Jesus. That is why He came. The world is not an exact representation of God. The church is not an exact representation of God. Jesus is. He came to freshly present what the Father is like to those of us who are spiritually impaired by a world of suffering.

The Tenderness of Jesus, in many ways, is my most personal book to date. I invite you to listen in as I write to my four young adult children about the tenderness of Jesus Christ. Come sit with us around the dinner table. May this fresh glimpse of Jesus heal your broken heart and reignite your spiritual fervor.

Soul Care

7 Transformational Principles for a Healthy Soul

Soul Care explores seven principles that can lead to lasting transformation and freedom for all who struggle with a broken, damaged, and sin-stained soul.

Brokenness grasps for the soul of humanity. We are broken body, soul, and spirit, and we need the healing touch of Jesus. *Soul Care* explores seven principles that are profound healing tools of God: securing your identity, repentance, breaking family sin patterns, forgiving others, healing wounds, overcoming fears, and deliverance.

Dr. Rob Reimer challenges readers to engage in an interactive, roll-up-your-sleeves and get messy process—a journey of self-reflection, Holy Spirit inspiration, deep wrestling, and surrender. It is a process of discovering yourself in true community and discovering God as He pierces through the layers of your heart.

Life change is hard. But these principles, when packaged together and lived out, can lead to lasting transformation, freedom, and a healthy soul. *Soul Care* encourages you to gather a small group of comrades in arms, read and process together, open your souls to one another, access the presence and power of God together, and journey together into the freedom and fullness of Christ.

The Soul Care Leader
Healthy Living and Leading

How do we live a healthy life and lead others into spiritual, emotional and relational health and wholeness? That is the focus of this book.

Trying to help others find freedom and wholeness is draining work. What do we do to become healthy and maintain our well-being? What are the practices and rhythms we need to engage in to be effective Soul Care practitioners? How do we create a culture where life-change flourishes? How do we minister in the power of the Spirit so we can lead others into breakthroughs?

Too often people are talking about the same problems that they were talking about several years ago, but they aren't finding a path to freedom. We need to help people get to the roots and not merely manage their dysfunction and sin. These are the questions and topics that this book will seek to equip you in as you seek to live and lead people into freedom and fullness in Christ.